WOMAN TO WOMAN

Woman to Woman

The Power of
Intergenerational Mentorship

**DR. VALERIA & RACHAEL
EDMONDS**

Copyright © 2025 by Rachael and Valeria Edmonds
All rights reserved.

Unless otherwise noted, scripture quotations are taken from the Holy Bible, New International Version®, and NIV® International Bible Society 1973.

PRINT ISBN 979-8-218-61719-6
eBook ISBN 979-8-218-61720-2

Cover Design by Jennifer Chester
Edited by Vera Linda

Table of Contents

INTRODUCTION	1
How to Use This Book	3
PROLOGUE: IN HER TEENS	5
TODAY'S WOMAN IN HER TWENTIES	9
Advice for Miss Twenty-Something	19
TODAY'S WOMAN IN HER THIRTIES	23
Advice for Ms. Thirty-Something	34
TODAY'S WOMAN IN HER FORTIES	39
Advice for Ms. Forty-Something	52
TODAY'S WOMAN IN HER FIFTIES	57
Advice for Ms. Fifty-Something	72
TODAY'S WOMAN IN HER SIXTIES	75
EPILOGUE: THE POWER OF WOMAN-TO-WOMAN WISDOM	93
A MENTORING GUIDE	95
Finding a Mentor	98
ACKNOWLEDGMENTS	101
ABOUT THE AUTHORS	103

Introduction

"And when you get to where you're going, turn around and help her too. For there was a time, not long ago, when she was you."

Author Unknown

As women, we are constantly evolving. Like Michelle Obama, we are becoming. Using a house as a metaphor for how we progress through different life stages, a woman in her twenties is establishing herself as an adult and laying the foundation for the rest of her life. In her thirties, she is building the house and creating a framework for living out her vision for her future, which often includes creating a family. In her forties, she may start to shake things up a bit and renovate her life, like you would a house, if it no longer suits her. In her fifties, she has lived long enough to be secure and established. She is focused on maintaining what she has worked so hard to build. By her sixties, she is starting to declutter by shedding unwanted things she has been holding onto and reflecting on the equity she has built up over a lifetime. One thing we know for sure is that "unless the Lord builds the house, they labor in vain who build it" (Psalms 1271).

One beautiful aspect of our transformation is the impact that other women can have on our lives. When we are open to it, other women can pour into us and become a part of our story. Those are 'the women who make us' who we become. While both positive and negative experiences shape us, we grow when we learn from them. Further, as we mature, we are in a position to share those lessons with others. Whether formal or informal, mentoring is a way to share our life lessons with others. It might be on the job, at home, or in the community, but having someone to guide you and help you overcome barriers is very beneficial. Unfortunately, not every woman has the benefit of an older or more experienced woman who shares advice or encouragement. Often, women have to learn things the hard way or through trial and error. However, that is not the way God intended.

Scripture says to "tell the older women to behave as those who love the Lord should. They must not gossip about others or be slaves of wine. They must teach what is proper so that the younger women will be loving wives and mothers. Each of the younger women must be sensible and kind, as well as a good homemaker who prioritizes her husband. Then no one can say insulting things about God's message" (Titus 2:3-5 CEV). Consistent with these instructions, Toni Morrison said, "Our friendships with other women are the currency of our lives. In the absence of so many support systems, we are it for each other." However, building these types of supportive relationships takes intentional effort, and it can be challenging when it comes to communicating across generations. Women of different ages have various priorities and ways of being in the world based on their life stage.

Recognizing that each decade brings new experiences and challenges as we strive to be all we can be, over the course of a year, we talked to over sixty women about their lives to understand today's woman and how she's evolving. Some were on the cusp of a new chapter, and some were right in the thick of it. The questions allowed each woman to reflect on the best thing about her life and her biggest concern at this stage. We also discussed her physical and spiritual health, love life, professional life, and relationships with older women. Each participant was asked to share the best advice she had gotten from an older woman in her life and share wisdom for younger women based on her life experiences. As a result of our conversations, we have developed six unique portraits of women at different life stages to help us all understand each other better.

How to Use This Book

This work is meant to be used as a guide for navigating life through different stages and mentoring across generations, believing we can all learn from each other. The book aims to empower women at every stage of life through shared wisdom and mentoring.

- You can read the chapter focused on your stage of life to see if it reflects your experience as you are evolving personally as a woman or if you can learn more about yourself and your peers.
- You can read the chapter on the next decade of life to understand what to expect as you transition to that stage.
- You can read the chapter focused on someone you mentor to gain a better understanding of how they perceive themselves and their challenges. Consider a woman in your life who is a mentee, and read the chapter to enhance your understanding of her.
- You can read the chapter at a later stage in life to better understand the woman with whom you want to build a stronger relationship. Consider a woman in your life who is currently a mentor or has the potential to be one, and read the chapter to gain deeper insights into her.

As you read the profiles of women from each decade, we hope they resonate, inspire, and challenge you to live a life that reflects our identity as daughters of a King. He has called us to walk together on this journey called life. We pray that this book fulfills its intended purpose: to help us lift others as we rise and to empower one another with grace and wisdom.

Prologue: In Her Teens

"You are altogether beautiful, my darling, beautiful in every way."

Song of Songs 4:7 NLT

Ms. Thelma pulled a simple red dress out from the back of her closet. "I sewed this by hand when I was just about your age," she said, her voice soft with memory. " It was for my first job interview."

Feeling overwhelmed and distracted by a school project, sixteen-year-old Savannah looked up from her phone and reached out to touch the worn fabric. It was cute, but she couldn't imagine getting that dressed up for an interview. "Did you get the job, Grandma?" she asked.

Her grandmother laughed, folding the dress carefully. "No, child, but that's not the point. My mom, your Great-Granny, couldn't afford to buy me something new for the interview, but she wanted me to look nice. She had been saving that fabric for something special. I don't remember what. But she told me to take that red fabric and make something pretty to wear. She had taught me how to sew and quilt, so she knew I could do it. She said, 'If you look good, you feel good about yourself.' Honey, I worked on that dress all night and walked into that office knowing I had done my best to look professional, and I was so proud of myself. The experience of creating something beautiful with my own hands taught me more than the job ever could. Since then, I have been doing my best to work hard and take pride in my appearance. I've always been confident in my ability and never let it bother me when things didn't go as planned."

Her words stayed with Savannah. She didn't know then that it would guide her through every season of her life and that one day, she would be the one passing down the wisdom of that red dress.

To every teen girl reading this, know that the advice you receive from the older women in your life, even the simplest of words, may someday become the red dress in your closet—the wisdom you carry forward when you need it most. Today, our Ms. Twenty-Something has a message for you, born from her experiences and lessons as a young adult, to help you navigate the twists and turns ahead. Her advice to you is:

Take Your Time

It's important to live in the moment and not try to rush through life. Focus on the present for a more enjoyable teenage experience. It's easy to get caught up in future worries, but know that the stuff you're worrying about now probably won't matter to you later.

Have Fun and Let Go

Your teenage years are a time to enjoy life without being weighed down by many adult responsibilities. Have fun, explore, and savor the freedom of being a teenager. Embrace life with playfulness and ease. Allow yourself to breathe, have fun, and don't take everything so seriously.

Stay True to Yourself

Move how YOU move, and have confidence in creating your own path. Embrace your individuality, and don't be swayed by peer pressure or external expectations. It's okay to focus on what genuinely moves you and not let distractions steer you away from what truly matters to you.

Explore All Your Options

Avoid limiting yourself to familiar surroundings or ideas. Remain open-minded and open to new perspectives. Be curious about the world and travel. Know that growth often happens outside your comfort zone - so bravely seek out new experiences and challenge your boundaries.

Balance Fun and Responsibility

You either 'pay now and play later or play now and pay later.' Consider the long-term consequences of your choices, but also remember to enjoy life. You have to make responsible choices that align with your long-term goals because hard work now can lead to greater rewards later.

Stand on Solid Ground

Focus on education, relationships, and personal values that will help you build a strong foundation for the future. Be careful about the people you associate with and make choices that will benefit you in the long run. Spend quality time with your parents and give them grace when you can. Having a solid base will help you navigate future challenges.

Give Yourself Grace

Be kind to yourself, and don't expect perfection. Embrace flaws and setbacks as part of the learning process, and know that personal failures are crucial for developing resilience and self-acceptance. You are better than you think you are.

You Don't Have to Have Everything Figured Out

It's okay not to have all the answers or a set life plan in your teens. It's normal to feel uncertain. It's perfectly acceptable to explore and adjust your path as you go. Self-discovery is a continuous journey that hopefully never ends. We are always evolving as women.

Today's Woman in Her Twenties

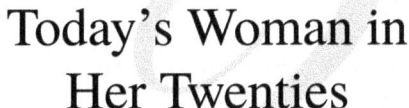

"Don't copy the behavior and customs of this world, but let God transform you into a new person by changing the way you think. Then you will learn to know God's will for you, which is good and pleasing and perfect."
Romans 12:2 NLT

A Foundation for the Future

"Come sit with me," Dana said, gesturing toward the empty chair beside her. "You don't want to eat alone on your first day."

Brianna hesitated, her lunch tray feeling heavier than it should. The cafeteria buzzed with the chatter of professionals who all seemed to know their place in this world—a world Brianna was just stepping into. She had barely made it through her morning orientation at the consulting firm and was already feeling overwhelmed.

Dana, a poised woman in her early thirties, smiled warmly, sensing Brianna's uncertainty. "I remember my first day. It was a lot."

Brianna exhaled, relieved by the invitation. "I feel like I have no idea what I'm doing," she admitted, setting down her tray.

Dana laughed. "None of us did at first. But I've been here for ten years—I can help you figure out the unspoken rules. My first supervisor told me that success in organizations is a combination of talent, image, and exposure. That advice has stayed with me and continues to guide me to this day."

That lunch marked the beginning of something Brianna didn't realize she needed. Over the next few weeks, Dana became more than just a helpful colleague—she became a mentor. She taught Brianna how to navigate office politics, advocate for herself in meetings, and interpret the sometimes ambiguous feedback from senior leadership.

One Friday afternoon, after an exhausting week of client meetings, Dana leaned over Brianna's cubicle. "I know you're probably tempted to go home and sleep all weekend, but you need a real break. Why don't you come over for dinner tomorrow? No work talk—just good food and some downtime."

Brianna hesitated. It felt personal, and she wasn't sure if she should cross that line with someone she worked with. But something about Dana's sincerity reassured her. She had made plans to hang out with her little cousin, Savannah, and didn't want to let her down. "Do you mind if I bring my cousin with me? I try to spend time with her on the weekends so that she can stay focused on getting into college."

"Of course! The more, the merrier. Hope you both like Italian."

The next evening, as she stepped into Dana's beautifully decorated townhome, Brianna realized that this visit wasn't just about food; it was about learning how to balance ambition with real life. Dana's husband greeted her with a nod from the kitchen, while Dana's toddler peeked at her from behind a couch cushion. The aroma of home-cooked food filled the space, a stark contrast to the takeout containers littering Brianna's apartment.

"You know, when I was your age, I thought success meant late nights and working harder than everyone else," Dana said, pouring them each a glass of sweet tea. "But real success? It's knowing when to close the laptop and truly live."

As they continued to talk, Savannah listened intently to their discussion about working in Corporate America. She whispered to her cousin, "Thanks for letting me come with you. I learned so much from you both. It really motivates me to stay focused on my schoolwork."

Brianna smiled and soaked in the warmth of the moment. She realized that success wasn't just about mastering spreadsheets and presentations; it was also about building a life—one filled with mentors who guided her, relationships that sustained her, and moments like this that reminded her of what truly mattered.

That night, as she left Dana's house, Brianna felt a shift. She wasn't just a lost twenty-something trying to prove herself in the corporate world—she was a woman at the start of something extraordinary, with someone to help her along the way.

*I*n today's rapidly evolving world, women in their twenties navigate a landscape filled with opportunities and challenges. This chapter explores various aspects of their lives, from personal growth and professional ambitions to the intricacies of maintaining relationships and financial independence. It delves into the concerns, joys, and advice that shape their experiences, painting a vivid picture of what it means to be a woman in her twenties today. She is establishing herself as an adult and focused on laying a foundation for the rest of her life.

Embracing Freedom and Autonomy

Ms. Twenty-Something is excited about this stage of life with its tremendous freedom and independence. She is in pursuit of autonomy as she embraces adulthood, and this desire manifests in every aspect of her life. She cherishes the liberty to express herself authentically, to carve out moments of solitude when needed, and to choose her companions wisely. The journey to financial stability plays a significant role in this pursuit, granting her the opportunity to travel, begin her career, and indulge in life's pleasures.

Family serves as a vital anchor in her life. Her family is the cornerstone of stability and reassurance, providing a support system that empowers her to explore new horizons. She finds satisfaction in maintaining a balance between professional responsibilities and the need for self-reflection, family time, and friendships. Her first home is her sanctuary, a place where safety, comfort, and personal expression are prioritized. Through her deliberate choices, she crafts a life of peace and fulfillment interwoven with a strong sense of independence.

> "FREEDOM IS GOOD, BUT IT'S A LOT OF RESPONSIBILITY."

Navigating Uncertainty and Ambition

Both uncertainty and ambition mark the journey through her twenties. Professionally, she feels the pressure to succeed and grow while grappling with the relentless march of time. There's a constant struggle to find enough hours in the day to achieve her goals, which can lead to anxiety about the future. Looming questions about career paths, life choices, and personal growth weigh heavily on her mind.

> "ADULTING NEVER STOPS. THERE'S ALWAYS SOMETHING!"

The transition from academic life to the workforce brings its own set of challenges. She has to navigate new roles, growing responsibilities, evolving friendships, and mounting financial obligations like rent and student loans. Establishing stability is essential, particularly if major changes like moving to her first apartment on her own or to a new city have unsettled her life. Mental and physical health becomes a focal point as she strives to maintain her well-being amidst what feels like chaos. Therapy and gym memberships are new priorities that allow her to function as her best self. Balancing her ambitions with the risk of burnout is a delicate dance she must master.

Yet, despite these challenges, she is resilient. Her twenties are a time of immense personal and professional growth, where the uncertainty of the future is met with determination and a willingness to adapt. This period is about more than simply surviving but thriving amidst life's unpredictability.

The Challenge of Adulting

Adulting presents a series of multifaceted challenges, chief among them being financial stability and independence. Ms. Twenty-Something struggles with balancing her budget and often lacks guidance in navigating her newfound adult responsibilities. She finds that making ends meet and saving for the future usually necessitates short-term sacrifices for long-term gains.

Entering adulthood feels like stepping into uncharted territory, where each decision carries potentially serious consequences. From maintaining friendships and mental health to contemplating major life decisions like home ownership and romantic partnerships, the responsibilities of adulthood require critical thinking and careful planning. Making friends and dating once you're out of the school setting is more challenging than she anticipated. No one told her where to go to make friends or how to run into Prince Charming casually.

> "ADULTING IS A SCAM!"

Ms. Twenty-Something is realizing that adulting is about evolving to meet the demands of an unpredictable future filled with potential. Fear of the unknown is a challenge she is facing head on.

The Sanctity of Personal Spaces

For Ms. Twenty-Something, personal spaces hold significant meaning and reflect her inner world. The cleanliness and organization of her home, particularly spaces like the kitchen or her bedroom, are often seen as extensions of her mental state.

She may prioritize her bedroom as a sanctuary for rest and rejuvenation. A tidy bedroom that is organized to reflect her personal style is not just about aesthetics but about creating an environment that fosters peace and tranquility. This space becomes a refuge from the outside world, a place where she can unwind and recharge, aligning her physical surroundings with her mental well-being. Similarly, the kitchen may be the highlighted space of control and comfort. It's a place where she can take charge, setting the tone for her home environment.

By maintaining order and cleanliness in her home, she creates a space that supports her daily activities and serves as a foundation for her well-being in more ways than one.

Spiritual Exploration and Growth

Her twenties are a time of spiritual discovery and personal growth apart from what was imparted to her as a child. This phase of her doctrinal journey is characterized by a departure from traditional religious frameworks toward a more personal, relationship-oriented approach to spirituality.

Ms. Twenty-Something often embraces the freedom to explore her faith independently and sometimes even question God. Engaging in practices like prayer, meditation, and occasional Bible reading can answer questions or leave her with more. Her spiritual journey is dynamic, sometimes feeling like a rollercoaster of connection and disconnection with a higher power. Motherhood, for those who experience it in their twenties, often deepens this spiritual connection, prompting reflections on beliefs in a higher power as a means of understanding her role as a mother.

> "I'M AT THE POINT WHERE I'M MY OWN PERSON, AND I CAN HAVE MY OWN RELATIONSHIP WITH GOD."

In her twenties, the emphasis often shifts from strict adherence to religious doctrine to a more personal relationship with God, which allows for growth and fulfillment amidst life's new demands. Despite the uncertainties of this season, she finds solace and stability in her faith, recognizing that she cannot navigate everything alone.

The Quest for Mr. Right

In the realm of romantic relationships, her concept of the perfect guy is still evolving. Ms. Twenty-Something may have initially had specific criteria for her ideal partner, often focusing on superficial traits like appearance and status. However, with time and experience with a few frogs, her focus shifts to his authenticity and true compatibility. "Mr. Right" is someone who shares her values, has a genuine relationship with God, and can make her smile even on the toughest days. Rather than a checklist of qualities, her

> "THERE'S A LOT OF LOVE THAT I NEED TO POUR INTO MYSELF BEFORE I CAN POUR IT INTO ANYONE ELSE."

instincts about true love are now based on a feeling—a connection that brings her peace and allows her to be her true self.

The ideal partner for her is not perfect, but he is someone who supports her growth and complements her journey. Whether he is tall and handsome or a gentleman who provides stability and happiness, Mr. Right-for-Her is recognized by the good vibes and ease he brings into her life.

Joy and Fulfillment in Everyday Life

Despite the challenges of adulthood, Ms. Twenty-Something finds joy and fulfillment in many aspects of her life. Her close-knit relationships play a vital role in her happiness, providing companionship, comfort, support, and laughter in everyday moments.

> "ALL I REALLY CARE ABOUT IS FEELING AT PEACE."

Personal interests and hobbies, like reading, music, and travel, serve as escapes from the pressures of her daily life. These activities offer relaxation and a chance to explore new things, which fill her cup with joy.

For her, the anticipation of future possibilities and the hope for what lies ahead provide motivation and a positive outlook on life. This sense of optimism and the pursuit of personal growth and self-discovery form the foundation of happiness for Ms. Twenty-Something.

Seeking Advice and Wisdom

Ms. Twenty-Something turns to trusted sources for advice and guidance when needed. Family members, particularly mothers and sisters, are at the top of her list of advisors, providing wisdom rooted in experience and understanding. These family ties offer invaluable support, whether it's help navigating life decisions or providing womanly advice.

College classmates and lifelong friends are also essential resources for diverse perspectives when she needs advice. These like-minded women provide a supportive network that can be relied upon for guidance on various matters, from career choices to personal growth.

Professionally, mentors play a crucial role in offering clarity and direction, helping Ms. Twenty-Something navigate work-related challenges with confidence. She is indeed fortunate when she finds someone at work who takes her under their wing and provides guidance for navigating the first steps of the career ladder.

> "SEEING ANOTHER'S JOURNEY DOES SOMETHING TO MY SPIRIT... I CAN'T DO THIS ALONE."

The collective wisdom from these trusted sources shapes her journey, offering support, inspiration, and practical advice to help her navigate life. Additionally, scripture reading and personal reflection provide a source of internal guidance, allowing for introspection and self-discovery.

Words of Wisdom from Older Women

Although she is young, she does listen. When older women speak into her life, Ms. Twenty-Something gets insights that have stood the test of time. One piece of advice she has taken to heart is to *"**never rush life,***" encouraging her to savor her youth and learn from others' experiences. This reminder to slow down and enjoy the present is a powerful antidote to the mounting pressures of daily life as an adult.

Advice regarding good financial judgment is a recurring theme she has encountered, emphasizing the importance of **making wise financial choices early on.** Practical tips, such as seeking scholarships instead of accruing debt for higher education, underscore the value of financial independence and foresight.

In relationships, she has been counseled to *"**choose your battles wisely,***" underscoring the importance of thoughtful decision-making and empathy in personal interactions.

She has also been cautioned not to fall into the comparison trap because *"**everything is not what it appears to be.***" Everybody's journey is different, and what is presented to the world is not the whole story and, therefore, should not be used as a measuring stick for her own success.

Ultimately, she has taken to heart guidance that encourages her to trust her instincts, do what makes her happy, and embrace life's journey.

Leaning Forward

In her twenties, she is a complex blend of ambition, anxiety, resilience, and self-discovery, navigating the uncertainties of life with a sense of independence and determination. Through the challenges of adulting, the pursuit of meaningful relationships, and the quest for personal growth, she blazes a trail uniquely her own. Her journey as a young woman is marked by a balance between freedom and responsibility, joy in everyday moments, and wisdom from those who have walked the path before.

This season of life is a time of profound transformation. As she leans into the next decade, the challenge is to allow herself to continue evolving and to appreciate small steps forward. Remember that none of the mistakes in her twenties will be wasted if she learns from them. She must commit to listening to the wisdom and guidance of God in His Word every day before listening to anything else. Then, commit to listening to the wisdom of trusted women in her life. She should seek godly wisdom from those who have been where she is going versus influencers who get paid for followers. She has to learn to ask for help when needed because the road ahead is not smooth. She should not go through life thinking she can make it alone but actively seek community with others. She should seek out mentors who align with her values, particularly in professional and personal transitions. Today's choices will shape her future, so this stage is an opportunity to create the foundation for a fulfilling life. It is up to her to become the woman she wants to be.

"Tune your ears to wisdom and concentrate on understanding. Cry out for insight and ask for understanding. Search for them as you would for silver; seek them like hidden treasures."
Proverbs 2:2-4 NLT

Wisdom from the Heart

Advice for Miss Twenty-Something

She has been where you are, and there were some things that women in their thirties wish they had known earlier. When asked to share advice for women in their twenties, they had plenty to share.

Embrace Exploration and Flexibility

"Your twenties are all about exploration—don't shy away from it. Embrace this season of your life with an open heart and mind. Be open to possibilities, and don't put too much pressure on yourself to have it all figured out. This is your time to experiment, try new things, and discover what truly excites you. Remember, it's okay if you don't have a clear path right now—this is your time to explore and learn."

Focus on Personal Growth and Self-Discovery

"This decade is about you—your growth, journey, and self-discovery. Ask yourself the important questions: 'What am I good at? What makes me happy? What impact do I want to have on the world?' Focus on yourself and your career. It's okay to be a little selfish right now. Trust that you're figuring it out and know that the process is just as important as the outcome."

Value Relationships and Seek Support

"Relationships matter. Invest in them, whether they're with family, friends, or mentors. Seek out people who make you feel safe and supported. Don't be afraid to be vulnerable; asking for help when needed is okay. Building a strong support system now will carry you through the ups and downs that life inevitably brings."

Embrace Your Unique Journey

"One of the best pieces of advice I can give you is to avoid the trap of comparison. Your journey is yours alone and won't look like anyone else's. Don't compare yourself to others—there's no 'right' timeline. The space you're in right now is meant for you. Be present in your own life, and trust that you are exactly where you're supposed to be."

Love and Resilience

"Love deeply, and don't be afraid to let yourself feel, even when it's hard. Yes, love until your heart breaks if that's what happens. Each experience will build your resilience and capacity for deeper, more unconditional love. The lessons you learn from love—both the joy and the pain—are invaluable and will shape you in ways you can't yet imagine."

A Prayer for Ms. Twenty-Something

Dear God,

Oh Lord, we praise You. You are excellent and worthy to be praised. We are so grateful for the freedom and autonomy that defines the woman reading this in her twenties. As she embraces the uncertainty and challenges of adulting, we pray that she keeps believing in You. We want to speak blessings and favor over her. Give her the courage to face the future with a sense of optimism and wisdom to make decisions that create a firm foundation for her life. Bless her as she seeks to establish herself personally and professionally. Watch over her as she blossoms into the woman that You created her to be. Remove her anxiety and replace it with peace, clarity, energy, direction and abundance. Please hear our prayer; we continue giving You all the praise and glory.

In the name of Your son, Jesus.

Amen

Today's Woman in Her Thirties

*"The wise woman builds her house,
but the foolish tears it down with her own hands."*
Proverbs 14:1 NASB2020

Building Her Life with Intention

Dana stared at the unopened moving boxes stacked in the corner of her living room, feeling the weight of everything she had yet to do. She had been working late with her sponsor, Brenda, to ensure she was on top of her game at work, but things at home were piling up.

A new house. A new job. A new baby on the way. And a toddler who didn't understand why his entire world had been uprooted. After ten years at her company, she was finally in a mid-level management role, had a beautiful home, and her husband, Chris, still adored her. She prided herself on being able to handle it all.

As busy as her life was, Dana enjoyed mentoring a bright new hire named Brianna, who reminded her so much of herself ten years ago—ambitious, eager, and slightly unsure. It felt good to invest in someone else and teach her the ropes. Dana was providing Brianna with the kind of guidance she had longed for when she was new to corporate life.

However, these days, she was exhausted before the day even started, bouncing between client meetings and chasing after a restless two-year-old in the evenings. When Sunday morning rolled around, Dana barely had the energy to get dressed for church. She almost stayed in bed, but Chris insisted. "You need this," he reminded her. "We both do."

That's how she ended up in the church foyer after the service, absentmindedly rubbing her belly while Chris went to collect their daughter from the nursery. She tried to will herself to go and fellowship with some of the other ladies. That's when she felt a gentle hand on her shoulder.

"Come sit with me for a moment, sweetheart," a woman said, guiding Dana toward a quiet corner.

It was one of the church's diaconates, a very sophisticated older woman who seemed to have it all together. Dana had attended Sister Evelyn's Sunday School class a few months ago and had always admired how poised and confidently she carried herself.

"You're glowing, but I see the tiredness behind your smile," Sister Evelyn said, studying her carefully. "Tell me, when was the last time you did something just for you?"

Dana blinked, unsure how to answer. Self-care? That was at the bottom of her to-do list.

"I'm just trying to keep everything together," she admitted. "I have a new job at work, my toddler is going through the terrible twos, and my husband, well you know that's just another person to try and keep happy—there's no time for me especially with another baby coming. I really wish my mom lived closer."

Sister Evelyn nodded knowingly. "That's exactly why you need to slow down and stop trying to be superwoman. You can't pour from an empty cup, you know. Your children and your husband benefit when you're taking care of yourself. Remember, your husband is going through this change with you. If you don't prioritize each other, life will pull you apart without you even realizing it. Trust me, I learned that the hard way."

Dana exhaled, her shoulders sinking as she let those words settle. "I barely have time for him, and frankly, I'm too tired whenever he tries to touch me."

Sister Evelyn smiled knowingly. "I understand. Frankly, you need to schedule time for romance just as you would for work commitments. Try blocking off an hour for yourself and an hour for your husband each week, and see if that helps. He will appreciate having quality time set aside for just the two of you. Also, if you need a sitter, don't hesitate to call me. I love children, and mine are all grown! I'd be happy to be the adopted local grandmother for yours."

That evening, Dana sat down with Chris and shared what Sister Evelyn had told her. Together, they made a plan—designating one night a week just for the two of them, even if it was just talking on the couch after their daughter was asleep. She also promised herself that she would start taking small moments for self-care, even if it was just a long shower with no interruptions or five minutes of quiet before opening her laptop each morning. She definitely planned to take Sister Evelyn up on her offer to babysit.

In the weeks that followed, things didn't magically become easier. The boxes still needed unpacking, work remained demanding, and parenting continued to be overwhelming. However, Dana felt lighter and more intentional. She knew she had support not only from her husband but also from an older woman at church. This meant a lot to her, especially since her own mother wasn't in the same city.

She was no longer just surviving; she was building—a family, a career, and a life that didn't just look good on the outside but felt good on the inside too.

As a woman reaches her thirties, she finds herself at the intersection of freedom, transition, and growth. For many, this decade marks a period of profound self-discovery and realignment of priorities. The modern woman in her thirties is navigating a unique landscape shaped by her experiences in her twenties, her evolving roles, and her vision for the future. The foundation has been laid; now, she is building her house and creating a framework for living out that vision.

Transitioning and Growing

Ms. Thirty-Something continues to enjoy an ever-growing sense of responsibility and clarity regarding what is important to her. This could be the result of significant career changes, the ability to work from home, or the personal growth that comes from life-altering events such as marriage, motherhood, relocating, or advancing in her career. For some, this realignment of priorities allows for more time with family, enriching her life with new layers of meaning and connection. She may also find this period conducive to personal reflection and self-discovery, leading to a deeper understanding of who she is and what she wants from life.

In her thirties, she is reshaping her identity. Whether through career shifts, the beginning of a marriage, navigating new phases such as motherhood, or finalizing a divorce, these transitions—though initially unsettling—are opportunities for personal growth. She finds peace in these changes by trusting the process and recognizing the lessons to be learned. In her pursuit of meaning for these changes, there is a sense that things are beginning to align, with divine guidance and a connection to a higher purpose.

> "I'M IN A TRANSITION PERIOD, AND I CAN TELL I'M BEING PREPARED FOR SOMETHING."

Career Journey

Career satisfaction in her thirties is truly a rollercoaster ride. At times, she may explore new fields, navigate transitions, or start entrepreneurial ventures. There may also be periods within this decade when she feels dissatisfied, stagnant, or unfulfilled. However, with prayer and dedication, she eventually finds satisfaction and success in her role. This satisfaction comes when her work has meaning and when she operates in her God-given gifts. When her career aligns with her purpose, it almost doesn't feel like work. Overall, things are going well, and she is grateful to have meaningful work. However, adjusting expectations and balancing personal priorities with career ambitions are key to her contentment.

Navigating Relationships

When it comes to love, Ms. Thirty-Something experiences a wide range of emotions and scenarios. She may worry about finding love, feeling the pressure of age and societal expectations. Her love life may be nonexistent as she waits for the right person, and that's okay. She spends her time preparing for future relationships by focusing on personal growth or simply enjoying her own company. Alternatively, she might be casually dating and going through a transformative phase, reassessing her needs and desires in the context of love and partnership. She may also find herself in a long-term, fulfilling relationship, enjoying stability, comfort, and contentment with her partner.

> "I DID A LOT TO SET MYSELF UP PROFESSIONALLY TO GET TO THIS POINT."

Whatever her relationship status, she only gives the same energy that she's getting. By thirty, the man in her life should be mature enough to match her commitment to putting in the work required for maintaining a relationship.

> "IF I'M GOING TO PUT ENERGY INTO SOMEONE, THEY NEED TO HAVE HUSBAND POTENTIAL."

Health and Well-being

Ms. Thirty-Something is trying to be more intentional about her physical and mental fitness, engaging in regular exercise and mindful living. But at times, she struggles with maintaining balance, particularly after major life changes. Sometimes, a major health event like finding fibroids, being diagnosed with a serious medical condition, or having a miscarriage can leave a lasting impact on her mind and body. Managing her physical health influences her choices and her activities. She is determined to move more and live a healthy lifestyle.

Self-care for her is multifaceted, encompassing both physical and mental health. At times, she experiences periods of high activity followed by crashes. She may struggle with sleep or feel overwhelmed after major life changes, such as having children. Because being in her thirties is often stressful, Ms. Thirty-Something recognizes the importance of managing her well-being, whether through setting boundaries, enjoying regular spa treatments, engaging in daily exercise, or simply taking time to rest and recover.

> "I'M CREATING BOUNDARIES WITH MY TIME, SAYING YES TO WHAT I WANT, AND DOING THINGS I LIKE."

Spiritual Growth

Spiritually, Ms. Thirty-Something is experiencing growth and renewal. She is reconnecting with her faith after periods of distance and is even exploring new spiritual practices. Whether it's through finding a new church, deepening her relationship with God through prayer, or maintaining consistent spiritual practices like devotion and intentional time in the Word, this decade often marks a significant period of spiritual reflection and development. If she is married, she is intentional about bringing her family along for the journey, including her children and partner, in her practice to help inform their understanding of God. Her spiritual growth is defined by their growth as a family.

> "I HAVE A STRONG FOUNDATION, BUT I NEED TO FIND MY RELATIONSHIP WITH GOD FOR MYSELF."

The Pursuit of Purpose and Flexibility

For Ms. Thirty-Something, everything is starting to make sense, and she can see her story coming together. However, her thirties are not without concerns. She is extremely busy managing her responsibilities while also contemplating what's next in life. The search for a career that aligns with her passions and skills often intensifies during this decade, as does the challenge of balancing multiple roles—wife, mother, employee, friend, daughter, sister, and more—while still prioritizing self-care.

> "I MADE A LOT OF FRIVOLOUS DECISIONS IN MY TWENTIES THAT I'M PAYING FOR NOW."

During this season, her desire for a purposeful life becomes more pronounced, especially if she has experienced a tremendous loss or has turned away from her faith due to church hurt. Ms. Thirty-Something is making choices that align with her priorities and purpose. She holds herself accountable for who she wants to become, but sometimes she fears that those around her may not accept or understand the changes she is making.

If given the chance, Ms. Thirty-Something would focus more on her personal fulfillment, freedom, flexibility, and meaningful connections. She dreams of becoming a published author, mentoring others, or simply having the time to live each day without rigid plans. She imagines a life of traveling and experiencing the world, whether it's exploring new places with loved ones or taking solo trips to rejuvenate her spirit. At home, she dreams of having more support, such as hiring help to manage daily responsibilities, which would allow her to focus on her relationships and well-being. Her fantasy is a life where she doesn't have to work so hard and can spend her days leisurely, volunteering and contributing to causes that fulfill her.

Finding Joy

What brings her joy? Family connections, personal fulfillment, creative pursuits, making an impact in her community, and engaging in leisure activities all contribute to her sense of happiness.

Whether she is tapping into her fun-loving side or simply being still, she is content wherever she can be her authentic self. Simple pleasures, such as a beautiful day, good food, or time spent in nature, bring her the most joy.

> "I GET JOY ANYTIME I CAN JUST BE MYSELF."

She gets deep satisfaction from the fulfillment that comes with helping others and the personal enrichment when experiencing "aha moments" of learning. Overall, the sources of her joy include a mix of personal connections, creative expression, relaxation, travel, simple pleasures, and personal fulfillment, highlighting a diverse range of things that bring her happiness during this stage of life.

Words of Wisdom from Older Women

Ms. Thirty-Something may not always have formal mentoring relationships, but she has a variety of women to whom she can turn for different types of advice. She might seek parenting and marriage guidance from her mother or aunt, career advice from her professional mentor, or everyday life support from her sorority sisters or spiritual mentors.

The wisdom she receives from older women serves as her guiding principles, like the importance of trusting in God's perfect timing. Ms. Thirty-Something is reminded to ***"trust God with all your heart and not rely on your own understanding because His plan for your life is not your plan."***

She is encouraged to prioritize self-reliance and independence whether or not she has the ideal romantic partnership, friendships, or career. Wise women advise her to ***"take care of yourself and always be able to stand strong on your own."***

In her relationships, she is urged to ***"live intentionally with yourself, your children, your husband, friends, family, etc."*** Intentional living fosters genuine connections and service to her loved ones with a full heart.

While she's bringing her best self to her relationships, she is advised to be kind to herself. ***"Give your all and do your best so you won't have any regrets."*** Older women advise that growth comes from making courageous decisions, even if they aren't perfect. They remind her to be kind to herself, trusting that she makes the best choices with the knowledge she has.

She carries with her the importance of understanding and self-governance. ***"Know what you're working with and govern yourself accordingly."*** She must be self-aware and make decisions that align with her circumstances and values while also accepting imperfection. ***"Perfection does not exist."*** Striving for perfection is futile, but embracing imperfection is key to personal growth and happiness.

Leaning Forward

Ms. Thirty-Something is a complex and multifaceted individual. She is navigating a unique challenge of prioritization, adaptation, and growth while balancing compounding concerns about love, purpose, and responsibility. She needs and desires the comfort provided by other women who support and guide her as life unfolds. Her life is shaped by her aspirations, career journey, physical and spiritual health, her growing family, and the advice she receives from those who have gone before her. Above all, she is focused on finding joy and fulfillment for herself and those she loves.

The reality she must face is that change is constant. As she navigates significant life transitions on her way to the next stage of life—whether related to career shifts, health, relationships, or motherhood—she should view these changes as opportunities for personal development and self-discovery. She must face her concerns and challenges head-on by practicing loving self-care and remembering that our trials come to make us strong. By focusing her energy on the few things that truly matter, she will be prepared for what God has planned for her. She must cultivate a "village" for support, whether that's finding mom groups, leaning on sisters, or reconnecting with friends.

Ms. Thirty-Something is building her house, putting up walls but selectively choosing the doors and windows to make room for transitions and traffic flow. As she leans into the next decade, she must actively and confidently work to establish herself as she becomes who she wants to be.

"The Lord himself goes before you and will be with you; he will never leave nor forsake you.
Do not be afraid; do not be discouraged."
Deuteronomy 31:8

Wisdom from the Heart

Advice for Ms. Thirty-Something

Based on her experiences, women in their forties remember their thirties as a time of struggling to manage significant life changes—marriage, motherhood, and career—which were all opportunities for growth. Her advice for those in their thirties resonates with lessons learned the hard way, and she shares it freely.

Practice Financial Responsibility

Start saving early and be intentional about how you manage your money. Being thoughtful about your financial future is crucial. Being proactive with money and investing will give you more freedom later on.

Embrace Joy and Faith

Don't be held hostage by a job or societal expectations. You can be bold, fearless, and full of joy. Become a friend of God and nurture your relationship by spending time with Him. Live your best life, knowing that joy is a fruit of the Spirit and the money will come when you live with purpose and enjoy the journey.

Be Patient and Trust the Process

Don't feel the need to have it all figured out right away. Allow things to unfold in God's timing, and trust that your path will reveal itself as you grow. It's important to know that it's okay not to have everything together at once.

Know Your Values and Set Boundaries

Determine what matters most to you—your values and deal breakers. Establishing firm boundaries is foundational for personal growth and will positively impact every area of your life.

Stay Open and Flexible

Don't be too rigid. Life can be unpredictable, and being open to new possibilities can bring unexpected growth. Learn from challenges and allow yourself the freedom to adapt. Life doesn't always go as planned, and embracing flexibility will allow you to discover new opportunities.

Live Authentically and Without Regret

Love yourself out loud. Show up as yourself and be you everywhere. Embrace what makes you unique. Identify what you truly want in life, separate from societal expectations. Pursue your dreams boldly because regret is often worse than failure. Trust in your ability to do anything you set your mind to, and don't be afraid to challenge the norm.

Pursue What Truly Matters

It's easy to be swept up in opportunities, but don't pursue them just because they're available. Focus on what truly matters to you and avoid distractions that don't align with your goals.

Prioritize Your Health and Well-being

Don't rush through life; enjoy the little moments. It's important to appreciate the present rather than constantly striving for the next thing. Be vigilant about your health and be kind to yourself. Make self-care a priority. Learn how to receive the love you pour out.

Do It Scared

You can do hard things! Don't let fear hold you back or stop you from doing things that matter to you. Face the challenges that come your way, and don't give up. Whether it's pursuing your dreams or making bold decisions, doing it scared is often the key to personal growth.

Stay True to Yourself

Always stay true to who you are. Even through life's changes, trust your intuition and beliefs. Embrace what makes you unique, and show up as your true self. Your authenticity will guide you to where you're meant to be.

Our Prayer for Ms. Thirty-Something

Dear God,

We come before You, lifting up the woman in her thirties who is reading this today. Lord, You know the desires of her heart, the challenges she faces, and the dreams she holds dear. We ask that You grant her clarity and direction as she navigates this season of her life. Lord, and make clear the purpose You have for her. May she walk confidently in the direction You have set before her, trusting that Your plans are for her good.

Father, we pray for abundance in every area of her life— abundance of peace, love, and opportunities. Fill her with Your peace that surpasses all understanding, calming her heart and mind amidst the busyness of life. Renew her strength and give her the energy she needs to fulfill her growing responsibilities and pursue her passions. May she find rest in You, knowing that You are her refuge and strength.

Guide her, Father, and help her find balance in all that she does. May she experience comfort, renewal, and revival in her soul. We pray that You place an older woman in her life—a mentor who can offer wisdom, support, and encouragement as she continues to grow in her purpose. Bring her joy in every season, Lord, and let her find fulfillment in Your presence.

As she goes through transitions and relocations, prepare her heart and mind for what lies ahead. Equip her with everything she needs to embrace the changes with faith and courage. Lord, may Your hand be upon her as she steps into new territories, trusting that You are with her every step of the way.

We thank You, God, for Your faithfulness and ask that You continue to work in her life, drawing her closer to You and unfolding Your perfect plan for her. May she find rest, renewal, and joy in You, today and always.

In the name of Your son, Jesus.

Amen

Today's Woman in Her Forties

*"Search me, God, and know my heart; Put me to
the test and know my anxious thoughts;"*
Psalm 139:23 NASB2020

Rehabbing with Wisdom

Brenda stared at the clock on her office wall—11:47 PM.

Another late night. Another dinner had gone cold on her desk. Another promise to herself broken.

She exhaled, rubbing her temples as she scrolled through emails. There was always something—another client needing last-minute revisions, another department crisis only she could solve. One email was from her protégé, Dana, thanking her for preparing her for a big meeting with senior management. Somehow, helping another woman break through the glass ceiling made it all worthwhile. Brenda actually welcomed the chaos; in fact, work had become her refuge, her distraction.

The divorce had left her feeling hollow. After sixteen years of marriage, she had walked away from the life she thought she'd built forever. The settlement was final, the house was sold, and her ex-husband, James, had moved on far faster than she had. Her kids were okay, but she worried about being there for them as a single mom. Work was the only place where she felt in control, so she threw herself into it. She had been busily climbing the ranks until she was promoted to Vice President six months ago.

But the long hours and relentless stress had taken a toll.

The migraine had started as a dull throb weeks ago, but last Friday, it hit like a freight train, followed by dizziness and a numbing fatigue she couldn't shake. When the doctor delivered the news—high blood pressure, dangerously high cholesterol, and severe stress-induced exhaustion—she barely heard the rest.

Now, sitting at her desk in an empty office, Brenda felt something unfamiliar creep in—fear. It seemed like God was testing her in every area of her life, and she was struggling to hold it all together.

She was lost in thought when she heard a firm but gentle voice behind her. "You're still here?"

Brenda turned to see Evelyn standing in the doorway. She was a senior consultant at the firm in her early sixties, with salt-and-pepper curls and a presence that commanded respect without needing to raise her voice.

"You're looking real tired, baby," Evelyn said, stepping inside. "You alright?"

Brenda forced a smile. "I'm fine. Just trying to stay ahead of the game."

Evelyn folded her arms. "Mm-hmm. That's what I used to say before I ended up in the hospital."

Brenda glanced down, guilt creeping in. She hadn't told anyone about the diagnosis.

Evelyn pulled up a chair. "Listen, I know what you're doing. You think if you work hard enough, you won't have to feel it. The loneliness. The disappointment. The loss. But running yourself into the ground won't heal you. It'll bury you."

Brenda felt the lump rise in her throat. "I don't know how else to do this," she admitted. "If I slow down, I feel like I'll fall apart."

Reaching over, Evelyn took her hand. "Then let yourself fall apart—for a moment. And stop working around the clock before you kill yourself. You need to establish some boundaries, honey. With this job. With these people. And most importantly, with your own mind."

Brenda closed her eyes. Boundaries? She hadn't had any in years. She had given everything—to her marriage and career—and now, barely anything was left.

"You don't have to carry this alone," Evelyn said softly. "Go home and talk to God. Really talk to Him. You've been holding all this in, trying to be strong, but He never asked you to carry this weight by yourself. You need rest, not just sleep—**real** rest. The kind only He can give."

Tears slid down Brenda's cheeks before she could stop them. Evelyn squeezed her hand. "You're not broken, baby. You're rebuilding. You have to trust that God's got you—even when you're not in control."

For the first time in months, Brenda didn't resist the truth in someone else's words. That night, she closed her laptop before midnight. She drove home in silence—no music, no emails, just her own heartbeat reminding her that she was still here.

As she lay in bed that night, staring at the ceiling, she whispered a prayer—not for strength to push through, but for the courage to stop, to breathe, and to let God lead the way.

Brenda began to delegate more at work and reconnected with God by spending time journaling each morning. When she spoke to her protégé, Dana, she confessed that she had become a workaholic and how it had affected her health and ruined her marriage. They had a very vulnerable conversation about setting boundaries and redefining success. Dana shared with her the app she used to plan quality time for her kids, her husband, and herself. It felt good to have an accountability partner as they both committed to prioritizing setting boundaries at work.

Today's woman in her forties embodies resilience as she navigates this pivotal stage of life. Midlife is generally a time of reflection and coming to grips with reality. Fortunately, Ms. Forty-Something is not afraid to see herself and her life for what it is. She ponders whether she has built her house on a strong foundation and whether or not it has good bones.

> "I'VE COME TO A POINT WHERE I ACKNOWLEDGE THIS IS WHO I AM. THIS IS ME."

This is a season of either questioning or validating her choices. She may begin to make some changes, like you would remodel or redesign your house if you find it no longer meets your needs. She may decide to refresh with a bit of touch-up paint or she may feel the need to do a complete renovation. She is in her prime and knows it's the right time to make necessary adjustments so she has the life she wants versus just the life she just gets.

On a personal level, she has embraced the journey of self-discovery, recognizing both her strengths and areas for growth while establishing healthy boundaries. Her accomplishments reflect her dedication to her family, career, and personal development, creating a fulfilling life rooted in purpose and belief in a higher power guiding her every step of the way.

The Best Part

For Ms. Forty-Something, the best things about her life are her relationship with God, her knowledge of who she is and what she wants, and her deep connection with her family. She finally feels like a grown woman! In her forties, she has found a harmonious balance between her career and personal life, allowing her to be present for her family while pursuing professional goals.

She has reached a place in life where she knows who she is and what makes her unique, embracing her true self without fear of judgment. She doesn't care what anyone else thinks because she has come to accept herself for who she is. The security she feels in her identity, purpose, and relationships brings her a sense of peace.

At forty-something, she is learning to lean into her strengths in every aspect of life. As a wife, love is flourishing as she enjoys deeper connections with her husband because they have weathered the inevitable storms. As a mother, she cherishes her children's health and well-being, recognizing the blessing of seeing them thrive. However, as a woman, she is still becoming.

> I'VE DONE A LOT OF THINGS THAT PEOPLE NEVER THOUGHT I WOULD DO.

Concerns and Challenges

In her forties, the concerns that occupy her thoughts are health, job security, and uncertainty regarding the future. She remembers once feeling invincible, but she now has to be more intentional about her well-being. Being mindful of her diet and regular exercise are essential to the long life she hopes for. She is keenly aware that unforeseen life events and challenges may force her to readjust and rethink her plans.

As she considers her future, job security and career goals are at the top of her mind. She grapples with decisions impacting her livelihood and those who depend on her. She's starting to think about retirement and what that might look like. Even if she's comfortable now, she knows circumstances can turn on a dime. She thinks about all the what-ifs, and it can get scary, but she doesn't operate in fear.

> "THE FUTURE SCARES ME BECAUSE I KNOW THINGS WILL CHANGE. I'M VERY COMFORTABLE NOW AND AFRAID TO BE UNCOMFORTABLE."

As a mother, she worries about her children's well-being and wants to be the mother they need. She wants to help her children while not overstepping, focusing on providing guidance and creating an environment where they can thrive and develop their sense of self.

Love Life

For Ms. Forty-Something, the love life is either poppin' or challenging, reflecting various relationship experiences. Whether being in love as a wife or finding love as a single woman, she knows that embracing love requires effort; it requires confidence in who she is, what she brings, and what she needs.

If married, intimacy has improved at this stage and emphasizes the importance of date nights and more intentional interactions now that her children are older. She has rekindled feelings for her husband, feeling giddy about their marriage again as they prioritize quality time together. Her marriage is stronger than ever, and her family dynamic is one of cooperation and support, energizing her as she grows as a wife and mother. She is celebrating milestones and acknowledging the ups and downs of her relationship. Ms. Forty-Something appreciates her partner's strengths and how they complement one another; they are a team. She recognizes that dual career pursuits have created challenges in her marriage. Yet, she remains committed to staying connected by prioritizing communication, continual dating, and regularly asking, "Do we still want to be here?"

Conversely, if single, she faces a challenge with dating and relationships at this stage because pickings are slim and some men seem intimidated by her success. Reflecting on her experiences, she recognizes the disparity between the reality of dating and its fantasy. She is a hopeful romantic who still wants a man who consistently pursues her. She struggles with the disappointment in past partners and the difficulties meeting potential matches in social settings, particularly within the church community. When the one she thought would be her life partner turns out to be a frog, she considers that "it might just be me." Her frustration has led her to consider a retreat from dating altogether. However, she worries about not having a partner with whom to face life's challenges as she ages.

Career and Ambition

Her career is progressing well, marked by gratitude for the significant achievements she has made so far. Ms. Forty-Something feels excited about her current role and the opportunities that have come her way, including advancement and new responsibilities. She relishes being viewed as an expert in her field and appreciates the chance to take risks and try new things at this stage in her professional life. Although she feels happy about surpassing her goals, she sometimes experiences disappointment for not pursuing her youthful dreams. She questions whether she has compromised too much of herself to get to this point. She is on the cusp of a new level and feels a healthy level of anxiety about making the best decisions for her career and the people depending on her.

> "I'M STAYING IN THE HOUSE MORE BECAUSE MEN ARE EXHAUSTING. I'M AT PEACE AND IF THEY ARE NOT ADDING THEN THEY CAN STAY AWAY."

Given the changes and upheaval she has witnessed, the one thing she knows for sure is that a long-term career with one company is not guaranteed. When it comes to the future, there are many unknowns. That is why she actively invests time in professional development to enhance her personal brand and stay relevant. She has navigated various obstacles as a working woman and is often still the only person of diversity at the table. Despite the stress that comes with increased responsibility, she maintains a sense of enjoyment and purpose in her work.

At this point in life, with retirement on the horizon, she focuses on finding contentment with her job and embraces the opportunity to prioritize family time over work responsibilities when she can. She is committed to continuous personal and professional growth as she navigates what may well be the apex of her career.

Health and Well-being

Ms. Forty-Something recognizes the impact of age on her health and well-being, prompting her to consider healthier lifestyle choices and manage stress better. She feels okay, although she is starting to deal with a few new health issues, and she has begun to focus more on fitness and weight management when she can find the time.

In her forties, she knows that addressing her struggles with poor eating habits and irregular sleep patterns will take discipline and self-awareness. She admits to neglecting her health in the past, acknowledging feeling overwhelmed at times and often running on fumes. She knows losing weight might be one way to boost her confidence and improve her physical health. However, finding time to exercise and maintain a healthy lifestyle can be challenging due to her busy schedule. Despite these challenges, she remains hopeful about making sustainable changes and plans to prioritize her physical health moving forward.

> "I NEVER HAD TO WORK OUT BEFORE, BUT NOW I CAN'T SHAKE IT. THE WEIGHT IS JUST COMING FOR ME."

Spiritual Growth

Ms. Forty-Something continues to benefit from the strong foundation she gained while growing up in the church. Her spiritual life reflects a journey of maturation shaped by intense personal experiences and challenges. Her faith has been tested in various ways, and there has been a significant turning point that ignited a spiritual awakening. Recognizing that you can grow up in church, but it may not grow up in you, she has seen significant improvements in her spiritual life through practices like tithing, fasting,

> "I WAS BAPTIST BORN, AND BAPTIST BRED. WHEN I DIE, I'LL BE BAPTIST DEAD."

and devotion. However, she has also faced challenges, especially following the loss of loved ones, which left her feeling disconnected. Yet, those experiences and breakthroughs have allowed her to reconnect with God. Now her relationship with God provides her with the reassurance that everything is unfolding as it should. She has moved from knowing God to trusting Him!

Her expression of faith has also evolved. Ms. Forty-Something is focused on returning to a spiritual flow by increasing her quiet time and engaging in prayer and devotionals. She and God are friends. Despite or because of the ups and downs in life, she acknowledges the importance of establishing a consistent spiritual routine and appreciates a church home where she can grow, serve in ministry, and find community. Balancing her commitments to ministry, like the praise and worship team, with her professional and family responsibilities has been challenging, but she is committed to making it work.

Mentoring and Community Support

Ms. Forty-Something actively mentors several women across various aspects of life, demonstrating a commitment to support and uplift those around her. Her mentoring interactions with younger women come in seasons or spurts, and it is often very informal. She has learned to adapt her approach, extending more grace in her relationships with younger women, providing guidance to her girlfriends, and offering support to her family members. Having been mentored throughout her life, she knows the importance of having supportive women and is committed to paying it forward.

Professionally, she is particularly dedicated to helping young women who share similar experiences or backgrounds because she can't teach what she doesn't know. Many of the women she mentors are beginning their careers, allowing her to share valuable insights and guidance. With more women looking to her for guidance now than at any other time in her career, she feels a strong obligation to support them.

Outside of work, she seeks to guide younger relatives and other women in her community, helping them understand the implications of their decisions. Her experience working with younger women has sometimes been emotionally challenging, especially as they navigate life changes that she hasn't faced herself. She has become a supportive figure, often referred to as an "auntie" by those she helps. By sharing her life experiences, she forms meaningful connections with younger women who often become friends.

Words of Wisdom from Older Women

Ms. Forty-Something turns to various sources for advice and support. First and foremost, she seeks guidance from the Lord. However, she also realizes that she must humble herself to listen and learn from older women. She consults different women for different needs. What she has learned from older women over the years is a rich tapestry of wisdom about all aspects of living.

She has been well advised that the foundation of a fulfilling life often begins with self-respect and advocacy. Knowing your worth means recognizing that "no" is a complete sentence. It's crucial to keep your boundaries intact and your priorities in focus. One wise woman cautioned against sharing too much, saying, *"Don't tell everybody your business—especially about your marriage. You will get over it, and others will not."* And above all, never settle. As another put it, "You don't want to be in a gilded cage and feel stuck."

She has also been advised that purpose often lies just beyond fear. One mentor shared, *"When you feel fear, purpose is near,"* reminding us that life's challenges can guide us toward meaning. Another said, *"God wastes nothing—it's not how you start, but how you finish,"* urging perseverance. Failure, while painful, is one of life's best teachers. Accepting setbacks graciously and moving forward is key. Another older woman advised, *"Don't be burdened by what has been, but on what should be."* And sometimes, striving for perfection isn't the answer: *"Sometimes, good is good enough."*

An older women she admired emphasized that faith anchors life's journey. **"God is in charge of promotion,"** one elder reassured, echoing the words of Jeremiah 29:11. One advised to *"let the moments of grief come and go,"* recognizing that loss is a part of life. Another warned, *"If you don't keep God first, everything else will crumble."* She has been reminded that integrity plays a vital role, too. *"Live a life you can be proud of by making thoughtful decisions with integrity,"* they advised, underscoring the value of authenticity in every choice.

She has been told that strong relationships require selflessness and care. Marriage, in particular, often means giving up something dear. *"A big part of marriage is giving up something that's important to you,"* one woman explained, sharing advice on preparing for partnership by practicing the art of sharing space. Family and marriage are fragile, *"a glass ball that can't be dropped."* Showing up for others is equally essential because "those that show up are sought after."

When seeking professional advice, an older woman said, *"work-life balance doesn't exist; it's more of a rhythm."* Time is our most precious resource—*"the great equalizer; it's how you use it that counts."* And never be afraid to seek help: *"Don't suffer in silence—raise your hand if you need help."*

"Be gentle with yourself," one elder counseled, urging a kinder approach to personal expectations. Amid life's demands, self-care is essential. Learning to center yourself early helps refill your cup so you can give more to others. And never forget your potential: *"Be great! You playing small does not serve the world."*

Lastly, she was counseled that preparation is key. Whether in life or love, wisdom lies in readiness. *"Establish a diverse board of directors to glean insights,"* one mentor suggested, emphasizing the value of seeking advice from trusted perspectives. An older woman once asked, *"How are you preparing yourself to be a wife?"* Her suggestion to practice sharing space served as a reminder that a successful partnership requires intentionality.

These pearls of wisdom inspire us all to embrace life's journey with courage and grace.

Leaning Forward

Today's woman in her forties navigates the complexities of family, career, health, and spirituality while remaining steadfast in her pursuit of fulfillment and connection. Embracing life's challenges and joys, she stands as a beacon of strength, ready to uplift others while continuing her journey of self-discovery.

As she leans into the next decade, she will be challenged to learn how to say no without feeling guilty and to remember that she can be generous while still maintaining boundaries. She must stop doubting her intuition and trust that God has equipped her for such a time as this. Ms. Forty-Something recognizes that wisdom is gained when knowledge meets experience, and that true wisdom comes from trusting God. It is time for her to shift her focus to mentoring more and to step into this role while balancing her responsibilities. She must make peace with all her past decisions and embrace the wisdom that leads her toward her destiny because it only gets better from here.

> *"Until now you have asked for nothing in My name; ask and you will receive, so that your joy may be made full."*
> John 16:24 NASB1995

Wisdom from the Heart

Advice for Ms. Forty-Something

Women in their fifties offer valuable advice to those in their forties, drawn from their own experiences, reflection, and overcoming challenges. Their wisdom encourages women to live intentionally, embrace their uniqueness, and prioritize what truly matters. Key themes emerge from their insights:

Live Fully and Be Present

"Show up! Enjoy every day as if it were your last." Life moves quickly, so make the most of the present without waiting for the "perfect" time. "Do all you can while you can… tomorrow is not promised."

Embrace Yourself and Your Gifts

Women in their fifties stress the importance of self-acceptance and authenticity. "Be comfortable just being you, and don't let anyone steal your joy." Remember, "You are beautiful! Whatever shape you are in—post-baby, older, whatever—you are still beautiful."

Set Your Own Course

Take charge of your own lives: "Let go of what others want from you," and "Figure out what you want." Life is too short to live for others' expectations. "In your 40s, you can still decide who you want to be."

Take Risks and Pursue Your Dreams

"Step out on faith and do whatever it is. God will find a way for it to happen for you." Embrace opportunities, take risks, and let go of fear because you're still young.

Keep Perspective and Find Balance

"Keep it balanced. Sometimes, we are so driven in our careers that we neglect other areas of our lives." Women in their fifties emphasize keeping Christ at the center and nurturing all aspects of life: family, health, faith, and personal goals.

Prioritize Health and Well-being

"Take care of your health because it will support everything else you do." They stress the importance of discussing changes like perimenopause with a doctor: "I thought the mood swings, headaches, etc., were just happening to me, and I suffered for years."

Build Relationships and Forgive

"Reconcile with anyone you've fallen out with. Forgive yourself. Accept love. Appreciate life. Be kind." Relationships and self-forgiveness are essential for peace and joy.

Define Your Legacy

"Be very clear about what you want your later years to look like. If you had to write your obituary, are you on a path to get there?" Reflect on your "why" and ensure your actions align with your goals.

A Prayer for Ms. Forty-Something

Dear Lord,

You are our rock and our salvation. You are the God of peace, and You are faithful. Thank You for the woman in her forties who is reading this right now. Thank You for her confidence in knowing who and whose she is. You have allowed her to accomplish so much, and we are grateful. We are excited about the impact she is making and trust that You will guide her steps as she seeks to do even greater things in her life.

Thank You for the tests and trials that she's been through which have made her strong and reminded her of Your steadfast presence in her life. We know that she has not always passed the tests, but she loves You with all of her heart. Let her know that her tests are to be her testimony and give her courage to do Your will and fulfill Your purposes. For we know that You have plans for her; plans for her to prosper and not harmed; plans to give her hope and a future.

We ask that You continue to sanctify her through and through. Bless her whole being - mind, body and and spirit. Give her peace and clarity regarding the future knowing that You are in complete control. When she is tired or overwhelmed, renew her strength and energy. Let her maintain her carefully balanced life with plenty of rest and self-care. Bless her family which means the world to her and keep them safe.

These and all things we ask in the name of Your son, Jesus Christ, knowing that the One who called her is faithful and He will do it.

Amen.

Today's Woman in Her Fifties

"Does not wisdom call out? Does not understanding raise her voice? At the highest point along the way, where the paths meet, she takes her stand; beside the gate leading into the city, at the entrance, she cries aloud: "To you, O people, I call out; I raise my voice to all mankind.

Proverbs 8:1-4 NIV

Embracing a Shifting Foundation

Evelyn stared at her son's empty bedroom, running her fingers across the smooth surface of his old desk. The walls, once covered in posters and college acceptance letters, now stood bare, except for a few forgotten thumbtacks. He had left for college three months ago, and though she was proud, the silence in the house was louder than she expected. With both kids grown, the house felt way too big.

Her phone buzzed with a text from her daughter. *Mom, I know you mean well, but I need to figure this out on my own. Love you.*

Evelyn sighed. It was yet another conversation in which she had tried to offer guidance, only to be met with resistance. Her daughter was thriving in her first real job, but Evelyn still worried—about her ability to make rent, her safety, and whether she was eating proper meals or just surviving on takeout.

She should have been prepared for this empty nest. She'd been balancing a demanding career while raising them to be independent and responsible. But no one told her that letting go—even when you had done everything right—would feel like this.

And then there was her mother. The once-vibrant woman who had raised her now needed her support—emotionally, physically, and financially. The doctor's visits, the prescription costs, and the home repairs her mother could no longer afford—all of it fell on Evelyn. With retirement looming, she felt the pressure mounting.

The only place where she still felt in control was at work. As a senior executive in her company, she had built a reputation for excellence. Evelyn was a well-respected and highly valued servant leader. She loved mentoring the younger women on her team, helping them navigate the challenges of office politics, male egos, and pushing against the ever-present glass ceiling. "You don't just lead here, Evelyn," her boss had told her. "You build people." And that was true. Pouring into others gave her a sense of fulfillment. She had staked her reputation on helping Brenda secure a key management position and was pleased to see her supporting other women.

But where was she in all of this? That Sunday after church, Evelyn sought out her spiritual mother for advice. Ms. Thelma noticed the strain on her face before Evelyn even opened her mouth. She listened quietly as Evelyn shared her list of worries and concerns.

"You're carrying a lot, baby," Ms. Thelma finally said, holding Evelyn's hands in her warm, steady grip. "The pastor just reminded us that as mature Christians, we should no longer be apprentices but experts at applying the Word to our lives. The Bible says to love your neighbor as yourself, which implies that we must take care of ourselves first. Tell me, when was the last time you focused on yourself and your future?"

Evelyn hesitated. "I don't have time for that. Between work, my kids, my mother—"

Ms. Thelma raised an eyebrow. "Your kids are grown. Your mother needs you, but she doesn't need all of you. And work? It'll be there whether you take a breath or not."

Evelyn sighed. "I just don't know how to step back. If I don't take care of everything, who will?"

Ms. Thelma chuckled softly. "Oh, sweetheart, God will. You're not supposed to hold everything together. That's His job. Yours is to live. It took me a long time to realize that I was the only one responsible for my happiness. Now I'm singing Angela Stone's '*I'm happy being me*!' and it's true.

Evelyn wasn't even sure she knew who she was outside of her job and being a mom.

"You've spent your life providing for everyone else. It's time to let go of some of that control and start enjoying what you've worked so hard for," Miss Thelma continued. "What are your passions? What lights you up?"

Passions? Evelyn had spent so much time making sure everyone else was okay that she had forgotten to ask herself what she wanted. After some thought, she answered, "I'm not sure anymore. Somewhere, I lost myself over the years."

Miss Thelma patted her hand. "You're in your prime, baby. Travel. Write. Dance. Go back to school if you want. And take care of that body of yours. Life is short, and you want to make the most of it while you're still able."

Nodding slowly, Evelyn let the truth of those words sink in.

That evening, she did something she hadn't done in years—she made a list just for herself. It included places she wanted to visit, hobbies she wanted to explore, and dreams she had put on hold. Now that she was approaching her sixties, she figured she should make her next chapter the best one yet.

She texted her daughter and simply said, *I trust you. Call me when you need me.*

She reached out to a financial planner to make a real plan for retirement—one that didn't include sacrificing her peace.

The next morning, she called and appointed Brenda as her delegate for the day. Instead of heading into the office, she took a

> long walk, breathing in the crisp air and reminding herself that she was still here. She had spent decades taking care of others. Now?
>
> It was time to start taking care of herself.

*T*oday's woman in her fifties embodies a unique blend of confidence, wisdom, and resilience. Having navigated decades of personal and professional challenges and growth, she stands firmly in her truth, embracing her individuality and priorities. This stage of life is a time of reflection and rediscovery. At fifty, her metaphorical house is comfortable and settled. She is now focused on maintaining the relationships and lifestyle she has worked so hard to build. Whether redefining relationships, thriving in her career, or giving back to others, she finds purpose in embracing the richness of her experiences. She is determined to savor every moment of the life she has built.

Ms. Fifty-Something's favorite thing about life is how much she has grown as a person. She exudes confidence, embraces who she is, and no longer hesitates to set boundaries or say no. Her competence shines as she leans into her expertise and boldly shares her insights at work and with her family. Her life is rich due to meaningful connections with those whose perspectives she treasures. Whether traveling, pursuing passions, or simply enjoying the freedom of focusing on herself without guilt, she embraces this season enthusiastically.

For Ms. Fifty-Something, her resilience is a source of pride. Having overcome challenges, from serious health scares to career hurdles, she is stronger and more grateful for each day. She cherishes her vitality and finds joy in staying active. She's excited about exploring passions such as traveling, writing, or ministry. She's bolder, grounded in her truth, and ready to face the future with hope and purpose.

> I'M BOLDER NOW THAN I WAS WHEN I WAS YOUNGER.

Navigating Challenges

The biggest concerns for Ms. Fifty-Something often revolve around preparing for her later years and navigating the transitions that come with this stage of life. She's determined to live her life to the fullest—adding value at work, spending meaningful time with loved ones, and witnessing her children thrive as adults.

Financial stability weighs heavily on her mind, whether she is preparing for retirement, adjusting to lifestyle changes, or ensuring her affairs are in order. She often reflects on whether she is being a good steward of her blessings and if she has done enough to set her children up for success. Aware that it is well past time for retirement planning, she is being hypervigilant about maximizing her investments.

Parenting adult children is a new challenge—she feels the weight of letting go, shifting her role to an advisor and friend, and trusting that the seeds she has sown will flourish. She has released them into the world while offering support when needed. However, she worries about the future her grandchildren will inherit, longing for a simpler, less polarized world.

> "I WORRY ABOUT THE THINGS I CAN'T CONTROL IN MY NEW ROLE AS A MOM WITH ADULT KIDS."

Whether supporting her children through their life transitions, caring for aging parents, or reflecting on her purpose, she is learning to adapt, let go, and embrace whatever lies ahead. Personal loss, such as the death of a parent, spouse, or dear friend, brings a complex mix of emotions as she adjusts to new dynamics of her life without them. While dealing with all the changes to her world at this stage of life, she is discovering herself anew. This self-awareness is exciting but daunting as she navigates what it means to move forward with her evolving identity.

Finding Her Purpose

For today's woman in her fifties, her sense of purpose and meaning often stems from her relationships, faith, and commitment to serving others. Her family is central to her reason for everything—being there for her children, grandchildren, or even parents as a caregiver anchors her life. She cherishes creating a legacy that ensures her ancestors would be proud. She finds joy in helping shape future generations as a mother, aunt, mentor, educator, or church leader.

> I'M IN A PLACE OF BEING STILL RIGHT NOW AND FOCUSING ON ME AND MY PURPOSE."

For Ms. Fifty-Something, this season is about rediscovery. After years of caregiving and self-sacrifice, she is now reflecting more on her life purpose and allowing herself the space to focus inward. She is redefining how she can best use her time, talent, and treasure. Whether sharing her story, addressing personal health goals, or reconnecting with her spouse more deeply–she is more intentional with her choices.

She views herself as a bridge, helping people navigate life's challenges in every space she occupies—be it work, community, family, or church. Whether she is pouring into other women, coaching leaders, or simply being present for friends, she strives to create meaningful connections in a world where isolation is all too common.

> ALL MY WORK IS FOCUSED ON HELPING PEOPLE IN EVERY SPACE I FIND MYSELF.

Her faith is often a guiding force, inspiring her to live a life that honors her beliefs and makes a lasting impact. Whether mentoring others, creating a safe and welcoming home, or being a moral compass for her family, she remains committed to leaving no regrets and living a life of eternal significance. Ultimately, her purpose is shaped by a determination to make a difference in the world around her.

Love and Relationships

For Ms. Fifty-Something, her love life is a nuanced and evolving part of her journey. Romance may have taken a backseat to personal priorities or life's transitions. However, there's an understanding that romantic love should enhance life rather than complicate it.

Her marriage is still a work in progress, marked by efforts to rediscover connection and rebuild intimacy. After years of busyness and maybe even unspoken resentments, she is working to communicate better and be more intentional. While it's not always perfect, there's a shared commitment to grow together and navigate this chapter with renewed purpose.

On the other hand, Ms. Fifty-Something may be embracing her singleness as providing space for self-fulfillment and peace in this season. Changing priorities, independence, and the complexities of balancing family expectations with personal desires add layers to the lived experience of a mature single woman. She acknowledges that dating can be challenging in your fifties, especially for those re-entering it after long relationships or marriages. However, finding a partner feels less urgent at this stage in life than living authentically and fully.

Ultimately, love in this stage of life is less about traditional relationships and more about self-awareness, honesty, and intention. Whether strengthening her marriage, finding joy in singleness, or exploring new relationships, she approaches love with the wisdom of experience and the courage to prioritize what truly matters.

Leaving a Legacy

After decades of hard work, Ms. Fifty-Something feels a sense of pride in her achievements and the legacy she's built. "I'm in my sweet spot," she reflects, describing how she's finally in a role that aligns with her strengths and expertise. Whether

> I RECOGNIZE YOU CAN ONLY BE RESPONSIBLE FOR YOURSELF. MY FOCUS IS NOW ON LEARNING TO LOVE MYSELF AND GOD.

reaching a long-held career goal, excelling as a leader, or preparing to celebrate retirement, she values being recognized for her contributions and making a noticeable impact.

This stage of life marks a shift for her professionally. Challenges still exist, such as navigating workplace politics or deciding to leave a role that no longer serves her while balancing her financial stability with her ego and emotions. Despite changing workplace demands, she continues to approach her career with determination, knowing she has the skills and resources to adapt as needed. Whether creating, consulting, or ministry—finding a new focus has reignited her drive. She enjoys projects or 'side hustles' that allow her to pursue her passions while still meeting the demands of her day job.

Retirement is looming. She sees the next chapter as an opportunity to find joy and meaning beyond traditional work. Having poured so much into her career, she feels she has earned the chance to step back, but that doesn't always mean stepping away completely. She plans to contribute meaningfully by volunteering, mentoring, or teaching, ensuring her skills and experience continue to make a difference.

> I'M REALLY CONFIDENT IN MY COMPETENCE.

Whether hitting her stride, pursuing new opportunities, or preparing for the next chapter, her career reflects her ability to grow, pivot, and thrive. With her legacy in mind, she focuses on mentoring others, leaving her mark, and ensuring that her work aligns with her values, capability, and passion.

Physical Wellness

For Ms. Fifty-Something, her physical health is a dynamic mix of achievements, challenges, and aspirations for continued well-being. Her health is good overall, but there are a few re-

> NOW THAT I'M STARTING TO EXPERIENCE SOME HEALTH ISSUES, I APPRECIATE EVERY DAY MORE.

minders of her age, such as aches, pains, night sweats, hot flashes, and changes in energy levels. Preventative care is increasing as a priority, with consistent physicals and screenings providing reassurance and a sense of control.

At this point in life, she has experienced serious health challenges that have taught her to appreciate her body and the importance of taking care of herself. She has had to make significant lifestyle changes, such as losing weight, improving her diet, and incorporating regular exercise, to regain control over their health. Whether through walking, yoga, swimming, or pickleball, staying active is the goal as she navigates hereditary conditions or seeks to avoid minor setbacks.

In her fifties, she is more in tune with her body, listening to what she needs and adapting her activities accordingly. She acknowledges areas where she could improve her physical health. Ms. Fifty-Something is focused on staying active, maintaining a healthy weight, and enjoying life.

Ongoing Spiritual Growth

Spirituality at fifty-something is profoundly personal. While her prayer life and relationship with God are strong, she still has areas where she desires growth, like consistency in church attendance or a deeper engagement with scripture. Her faith remains a cornerstone, helping her navigate work challenges, relationships, and life transitions.

Disruptions of recent years have shifted how she worships, with online ministries now offering her the inspiration needed for the week. She enjoys the ability to experience ministry and biblical teaching from multiple avenues. Yet, there remains an appreciation for the fellowship and community of a local church. This desire for belonging motivates her to continue with corporate worship, even as she acknowledges the imperfections of any church setting.

Her spiritual practices are varied and meaningful. She generally starts her days with devotion, maintains an active dialogue with God through prayer, and turns to scripture for guidance. She describes her spirituality as "growing" because her faith journey hasn't always been smooth. Questions about doctrine, past church experiences, and struggles with comparison have impacted her spiritual walk. Yet, these experiences have ultimately deepened her understanding of God and confidence in His plan.

Ms. Fifty-Something credits God for her resilience and joy in the face of adversity. She has learned to trust His timing, rely on His word, and draw closer to Him through life's uncertainties. Ultimately, her spiritual life is marked by an ongoing commitment to grow in her relationship with Christ. Her faith provides strength, guidance, and a sense of a higher purpose for her life.

Finding Joy

For Ms. Fifty-Something, 'joie de vivre' (i.e., the joy of life) comes from various things, big and small, and is often rooted in connection, fulfillment, and appreciation for life's blessings. Family is her primary source of happiness—spending time with loved ones, seeing children and grandchildren thrive, and enjoying authentic relationships bring deep satisfaction. Laughter brings light to her life.

Her joy also comes from helping others and witnessing their success. Whether guiding a student, mentoring someone in ministry, or serving others, seeing people reach their goals and thrive provides a profound sense of purpose and happiness. She finds it fulfilling to give back and make a difference in a world that sometimes feels self-centered.

> I CHERISH BEING AT PEACE BECAUSE I KNOW HOW QUICKLY IT CAN BE LOST.

She finds pleasure in meaningful conversations and authentic connections with like-minded people. Travel, the arts, and learning new things bring her excitement and adventure, while quiet moments of peace and reflection offer her contentment. From marveling at nature's beauty to reading a good book or savoring delicious food, the small pleasures of life are treasured. She cherishes peace, good health, and feeling comfortable in her skin because these are fragile and invaluable.

Whether enjoying the serenity of the beach, the thrill of a high-end restaurant, or the satisfaction of a job well done, she finds happiness in living fully and appreciating the richness of everyday experiences. For her, joy isn't just about being alive—it's about truly living.

Lifting Others

Ms. Fifty-Something sees mentorship as a natural extension of her life experiences. Whether formally or informally, she uplifts and guides others, sharing wisdom gained from her own journey. She knows that she can only teach what she knows, and people gravitate toward her who have similar interests, challenges, or goals. Whether through formal programs, informal relationships, or chance encounters, she uses the wisdom and knowledge she has gained from her life experiences to make a difference in the lives of other women.

> MY JOB NOW IS TO BE A GUIDE AND SHARE MY THOUGHTS BASED ON WHAT I WISH SOMEONE HAD TOLD ME.

In the workplace, she often serves as a mentor or sponsor, guiding younger colleagues, interns, or women transitioning into leadership roles. She sees their potential and offers coaching, advice, and encouragement to help them navigate challenges and seize opportunities. Beyond professional settings, she connects with younger family members, like cousins, nieces, her goddaughters, and her daughter, offering life advice and sharing her experiences. Her role as a mentor also extends to her community and church. Whether working with younger women dealing with grief or divorce, guiding young moms in children's ministry, or supporting young wives in a marriage class, she uses her life experiences to encourage others.

For her, mentoring isn't just about providing solutions—it's about listening, building trust, and fostering growth. Some of her mentoring relationships span years, evolving as her mentees grow and face new stages of life. Whether formally or informally, she is committed to being a guide, a sounding board, and a source of encouragement, knowing her insights from past experiences can help others thrive in ways she wishes someone had done for her.

A Trusted Village

For today's woman in her fifties, advice and support come from various trusted sources, carefully chosen based on the situation and the level of trust she feels. She values having a "village" of women who can pour into her life, whether for professional guidance, spiritual grounding, or personal encouragement. This village might include family members like her mother, sister, or aunt; a godmother or close friends she's known for decades; and mentors or colleagues who provide insight and direction.

Her friendships play a crucial role in her support system. Girlfriends from childhood, college, or professional circles are often her first call because she can be vulnerable and transparent. These friendships are built on trust, shared experiences, and a deep understanding of one another. She knows they will tell her what she needs to hear versus what she wants. Whether through group chats, annual trips, or one-on-one conversations, these relationships are a source of encouragement, laughter, and honesty.

Professionally, she seeks advice from past and present mentors who have helped shape her career. She may also turn to colleagues or peers for input, particularly those who understand her field or business. While finding supportive women in professional spaces hasn't always been easy, she values those who have mentored her and helped her navigate challenges.

Spiritually, her connection to God is a foundation for decision-making. She first turns to prayer and quiet reflection to seek guidance, trusting that God will direct her to the right person or answer when needed. Ministers or spiritual mentors in her church community are valuable sources of wisdom and strength.

While she treasures her support network, she is selective about who she confides in. Past experiences of hurt or judgment have taught her the importance of trusting only those who provide love, honesty, and a nonjudgmental ear. Her circle is small but deeply meaningful, providing the grounding she needs to face life's challenges with confidence and grace.

> IT'S HARD TO MAKE FRIENDS AT THIS AGE AND TRUST THEM WITH YOUR PERSONAL LIFE.

Words of Wisdom from Older Women

The advice given to Ms. Fifty-Something by the older women in her life has provided a rich blend of practical guidance, spiritual insight, and life lessons rooted in experience. They cautioned her to **never let others define her worth, to live authentically, and to hold fast to her independence**—financially, emotionally, and personally. A key piece of advice was to "***always have her own money, house, and car,***" ensuring she can navigate life's challenges with confidence and self-reliance. She was also encouraged to "***make self-care a priority***," nurturing her physical, emotional, and spiritual health. Her wise elders taught her that she is better equipped to care for others and fully enjoy life by taking care of herself.

Spiritually, older women urged Ms. Fifty-Something to "***put God first***" and to "***listen more to Him than to people.***" They advised her to "***pray and let it go,***" encouraging her to trust divine guidance over external influences.

Professionally, she was reminded that "***your work will speak for itself,***" underscoring the importance of integrity and preparation. Coupled with this was a cautionary note to think long-term, as "***you can't finance retirement***," highlighting the need for early financial planning and fiscal responsibility.

The value of meaningful relationships is another cornerstone of the advice she received. An older woman stressed the importance of choosing her circle wisely and keeping a small, trustworthy group of true friends who bring positivity and support into her life. "***Be present with loved ones***," was encouraged, reminding her that quality time is irreplaceable.

An older woman urged her to savor the special moments, make decisions purposefully, and move forward without regret. She was counseled, "**Don't start anything you're unwilling to keep up or finish**," and "**Don't rush to the next thing without enjoying where you are**," emphasizing the importance of living fully in the present.

Practical advice, such as **"pay your bills and repay loans first" and "invest wisely,"** encouraged her to plan with care and intention. These lessons reflect the importance of discipline, responsibility, and follow-through in building a life of stability and fulfillment.

Leaning Forward

Today's woman in her fifties is vibrant, introspective, and resilient. Ms. Fifty-Something has been through the fire and refined by it. She is no longer an apprentice in her faith; her lifestyle reflects her relationship with God and her knowledge of his Word. She faces life with wisdom gained from experience, prioritizing what truly matters and embracing each day with grace and purpose. Her journey is a testament to the strength, adaptability, and joy that define this remarkable stage of life.

In her fifties, she is finally free from striving and trying to make her way. She doesn't just look good and sound good; she does good. She knows her worth and thrives on her hard-earned respect. As she leans into her strengths and focuses on leaving a legacy personally and professionally, she must remember to prioritize her physical and spiritual health while embracing new adventures with the boldness that defines her. She must focus on giving back through intentionally sharing her wisdom by teaching at church, leading community initiatives, or mentoring younger colleagues. With decades of experience behind her, she can step into the next season, ready to savor its richness, embrace its challenges, and leave a lasting impact on those around her.

> *"When she speaks, her words are wise, and she gives instructions with kindness."*
> Proverbs 31:26 NLT

Wisdom from the Heart

Advice for Ms. Fifty-Something

Reflecting on her experience, Ms. Sixty-Something realizes that your fifties are the time to lean fully into who you are, embracing the wisdom, experience, and self-awareness gained through life's journey. Your fifties are not the season for grinding, struggling, or trying to prove yourself. Instead, it's time to step back, reflect on your accomplishments, and live with intentionality and joy. Her advice for you is to:

Embrace Who You Are

- Accept yourself as God made you, and believe who He says you are—not who you or others think you should be.
- Let go of worrying about what others think and competing with younger generations. Embrace the aging process, including its physical changes, with grace.
- Take care of your health—body, mind, and spirit. Eat well, stay active, and prioritize regular checkups. Shore up your spirituality to armor yourself against challenges, and seek support when needed, whether through therapy or a trusted community.

Live with Intention and Joy

- Be present in every moment and stop rushing to the next thing. There is power in being intentional and fully engaged in life.
- Let go of grudges and repair relationships. Forgiveness frees you to live without regret.
- Invest in the people who matter most, giving them the best of you instead of leftovers. Whether it's your spouse, family, or friends, prioritize making meaningful connections and deposits into these relationships.

Pursue What Brings You Fulfillment

- Focus on the things that bring you joy and happiness. Don't wait for others to make you happy—find joy within yourself and take it into your relationships and work.
- If you're in a job or relationship that doesn't serve you, have the courage to make a change. Vet the people in your life, set boundaries, and don't be afraid to disrupt the status quo.
- Understand God's purpose for your life and pursue it with everything you have. Trust that He has prepared and equipped you for what lies ahead.

Enjoy the Process

- This is the most exciting time of your life—live out loud and boldly. Try new things, learn something every day, and explore the world around you.
- Make a plan for the future, including retirement and end-of-life decisions so that you can enjoy the present with peace of mind.
- Don't sweat the small stuff—most things are small. Allow yourself grace, trust God's timing, and let your journey unfold.

A Prayer for Ms. Fifty Something

Dear God,

Oh Lord, You are great and greatly to be praised. You are everlasting and Your ways are too lofty for me. You don't faint or grow weary and You are unwavering in Your devotion to us. Lord, we thank You for the woman in their fifties who is reading this book and for Your steadfast presence in her life. We thank You for her testimony of all You have brought her through because we know that our trials come to make us strong. We pray that as she plans for her future, that You order her steps so that she has peace of mind. We pray that she uses her wisdom gained from experience to mentor other women and leave a lasting legacy. Give her the courage to share her testimony of Your goodness and mercy. Put other women in her path who could benefit from what she has to share. We praise You in advance for the lives she will touch and the legacy she establishes.

In the name of Your son, Jesus.

Amen

Today's Woman in Her Sixties

"The righteous will flourish like a palm tree, they will grow like a cedar of Lebanon; planted in the house of the Lord, they will flourish in the courts of our God. They will still bear fruit in old age, they will stay fresh and green."
- Psalm 92:12-14

A Lasting Legacy

Thelma had played the game well. She had fought for her seat at the table when the room was full of men who underestimated her. Through layoffs and promotions, glass ceilings, and silent victories, she had mastered the corporate world. She learned when to fight when to pivot, and when to let silence do the talking. She had swallowed her anger when her ideas were dismissed, only to be praised when echoed by someone else. She had smiled through the microaggressions, nodded through the patronizing comments, and worked twice as hard for half the recognition and rewards. And still, she rose.

Now she sat on the back deck of the home she had worked so hard for, letting the warmth of the sun kiss her face. The sweet smell of honeysuckle mixed with the faint aroma of soft rain. She exhaled deeply, pressing her bare feet into the cool wood, remembering a time when she wouldn't have dared to go outside in the rain. She wouldn't have risked wetting her hair or allowed herself to simply be. But now? Now, she danced in the rain.

The triumphs and setbacks had all led her here—her forever home. Semi-retirement had come as both a relief and a reckoning. She was grateful for the time to breathe, to dream, to just be. Yet, there were moments—like today—when the weight of it all caught up with her. Thelma sat there, lost in quiet musings.

She had lost her mother a few months ago. It wasn't unexpected, but grief had a way of creeping up on her when she least expected it—when she reached for the phone to tell her something or when she caught herself humming one of her mother's favorite gospel songs. That song, "Sometimes I Feel Like a Motherless Child," was now all too real for her.

And church? Now that was complicated.

The place where she had worshiped for decades no longer felt like home. The messages felt disconnected, and the community felt unfamiliar. There had been a split in the church that left her bereft. The new pastor was young and still learning how to lead. He was making many changes and hadn't appointed any women to key positions. After a lifetime of fighting to be seen in corporate America, she wasn't about to sit in a place where her spirit felt invisible.

So, where did she belong now?

She sipped her tea, rocking slowly, letting the rhythm settle her thoughts. Maybe this was an opportunity. Maybe, instead of looking for a community that fit her old self, she needed to build one for the woman she was now.

She planned to start with her sisters—not by blood, but by choice. The women who had fought the same battles carried the same burdens. Women who had been her prayer warriors, laughing partners, who reminded her of who she was when she forgot.

Thinking that the women at her old job might benefit from a sister circle, she called one of her mentees, Evelyn. "I'm inviting a group of women over for tea and testimony this weekend. I would love for you to come and bring one of your mentees with you. I think it would be good for us to share our stories and learn from each other."

Evelyn was pleasantly surprised. "Wow! I've been praying for an opportunity to work on women's empowerment. I want to remind women that we belong in every space we enter. This sounds like an answer to my prayers and a good place to start."

"Well, I look forward to seeing you. Don't forget to bring someone with you." Evelyn was sure that this was confirmation

Thelma had enjoyed the time with her granddaughter, Savannah, who visited during the holidays. It felt good to share her stories and discuss the lessons she had learned from her mother. So, she reached out to invite Savannah and a friend as well. These connections would provide her and other older women with opportunities to learn from the younger generations.

> The gathering that Saturday was everything Thelma had hoped it would be. Then, on Sunday, she tried a new church. The music was different, and the people were unfamiliar, but she allowed herself to sit in it and be open. Life had taught her that home wasn't always a place—it was a feeling. She was reminded that through every battle, every triumph, every tear, and every joy, God had never left her. After the service, the young lady next to her smiled and said, "It was nice worshiping with you today. You remind me of my mother." Thelma smiled, knowing this was the Holy Spirit putting someone in her path to remind her that she still had many opportunities to share her wisdom.
>
> As she left, Thelma smiled as a gentle breeze lifted her hair. The sun was out. And she was still standing.

For Ms. Sixty-Something, the best thing about life is the freedom, joy, and contentment she has found in this season. She is confident in her purpose, her capabilities, and the wisdom God has given her. Life has not been a crystal stair. Having weathered many storms, she often reflects in awe on having come this far. She is grateful for where she is and excited for where she's going. She cherishes the flexibility and resources that allow her to spend quality time with family and friends. Her literal and figurative house is well established and she has settled into it. With fewer responsibilities at this stage of her life, decluttering her mind, body, and home is now a priority. She needs to make space to pour into her loved ones, care for herself, and cultivate meaningful passion projects.

There is a profound joy for her in the simple things—moments of stillness, quiet reflection, and walks in nature that bring her peace and happiness. Having lived through the hectic years of raising children, working hard, and serving in the community, she treasures the slower pace that allows her to truly enjoy life.

> "THE FUNNY THING IS THIS WASN'T MY PLAN. THIS ISN'T WHAT I THOUGHT MY LIFE WOULD LOOK LIKE AT THIS STAGE, BUT IT'S EXACTLY WHAT I NEEDED."

Now in her sixties, she enjoys the freedom to choose how she spends her time, embracing life without the pressure to meet others' expectations. She is intentional about how she shows up and who she connects with, trusting the process and finding contentment in every situation. Her growing relationship with Christ provides her clarity, direction, and a constant reminder that God is in control.

Retirement plans have brought her a sense of liberation. For the first time in her adult life, she won't be tied to a job or busy raising children. Knowing that not everyone gets to this point is a privilege and a blessing to be at this stage of life. She's embracing this blessing by

> "I HAVE THE FREEDOM TO DO WHATEVER I WANT, AND I HAVE A CIRCLE OF PEOPLE IN MY LIFE THAT I LOVE AND ENJOY."

exploring new opportunities and carefully considering her commitments. There is an intentional shift from hard work to heart work.

Whether spending time with family, enjoying her circle of friends, volunteering in the community or simply living each day to the fullest, she feels immensely grateful.

Anxious for Nothing

Ms. Sixty-Something doesn't worry, she prays. The things she prays for reflect her love for family, the depth of her friendships, the realities of aging, and her desire to leave a meaningful legacy. She thinks about fulfilling the calling on her life and finishing well, knowing her years

> "IF YOU WORRY, DON'T PRAY, AND IF YOU PRAY, DON'T WORRY."

ahead are fewer than those behind her. While she trusts God's timing, she wants to make the most of the rest of her years on this earth. She is living intentionally and creating memories and lessons that will inspire her children and grandchildren. The question of what her legacy will be—what her epitaph might say—drives her to live without regrets.

Ms. Sixty-Something is concerned about the health and safety of her family, praying constantly for her children, grandchildren, and mother. She thinks about the world her children are navigating, with its rapid technological changes and the increasing distractions of modern life.

Her financial outlook is key to many decisions at this stage, particularly as the threshold for how much is needed to retire comfortably keeps moving. The reality of still having a mortgage weighs on her mind. However, she trusts God for His provision and is intentional about how she spends.

As she grows older, she is increasingly aware of the challenges this stage of life brings. Grief is a familiar companion, as she experiences the loss of friends and family. She remembers her mother saying, "Everybody around me seems to be dying," and now she understands the weight of those words. Yet, she has learned to let the grief wash over her, giving thanks for the time she's had with loved ones and not leaving anything unsaid.

Finding Purpose in Service

For Ms. Sixty-Something, her life finds purpose and meaning in being of service. At this stage, she feels called to pour into the lives of others, sharing the wisdom and experiences she has gained over the years. She finds joy in guiding others through mentoring, teaching a bible class, or creating a safe space for women to unburden themselves through her ministry service. She finds joy in helping women feel less alone in their struggles. She knows her journey and testimony can inspire others to thrive and strengthen their faith.

Much of her energy is devoted to making life better for her loved ones, providing guidance, and being a source of wisdom and encouragement. She cherishes the deep, abiding love of family and strives to play a supportive role for her adult children and grandchildren. Her role as a wife also brings meaning, as she works alongside her husband in ministering to others.

The many tests and trials she has faced over the years have made her strong. By the age of sixty, she realizes that every challenge she encounters is for her growth and ultimately for sharing with others as part of her testimony. Trusting that the one who has brought her this far won't leave her, she faces each day with courage and confidence. She follows the prompting of the Holy Spirit, praying on the spot for those in need and offering practical advice for navigating life's challenges.

> "I WANT TO BE THE PERSON I WISH SOMEONE HAD BEEN FOR ME."

Ms. Sixty-Something finds genuine satisfaction in serving her community. Through volunteering, mentoring, and supporting programs in low-income areas, she seeks to make a difference in the lives of others. She intentionally builds connections with other women, fostering growth and support. Whether helping someone find a home, offering encouragement, or simply being present, she knows her contributions matter.

Ultimately, Ms. Sixty-Something finds meaning in love, service, and obedience to her heavenly Father, knowing that each act of kindness reflects her purpose.

A Different Notion of Love

Whether she's been married for decades, divorced and remarried, in a situationship, or it's battery-operated, love means something different at sixty-something. Over the years, other priorities have taken more of her attention and influenced how she loves and perceives love. For her, love relates to a physical, emotional, and spiritual intimacy—where someone can truly "see into me." While passion may no longer take center stage as it once did, she values the connection and pleasure it brings. She is still a woman and no part of her dead or incapacitated. She cherishes the love, joy, and happiness that romantic relationships can offer.

A deeper friendship and the ability to be vulnerable in communication are what she treasures most in her relationship. At this stage, she has learned to clearly communicate her needs and advocate for herself, fostering equality and mutual respect in her relationship. She sees love as being present for one another, supporting each other through life's ups and downs, and finding joy in the quiet, simple moments.

For some, love at this stage is about rediscovering joy after loss. As a widow, divorcee, or mature single, Ms. Sixty-Something may choose to enter an unconventional romantic relationship and feel no obligation to explain her choices to others. She understands the rarity of finding love again and appreciates it when it happens, but she is equally comfortable embracing the peace and independence of single life. Companionship at this stage may include traveling with a partner or sharing bucket-list experiences with friends rather than adhering to the traditional model of romantic relationships. She knows that, at its core, love is less about convention and more about connection, authenticity, and joy.

> "LOVE IS PHYSICAL, EMOTIONAL, AND SPIRITUAL INTIMACY."

Ms. Sixty-Something also acknowledges the challenges of love. Whether navigating a situationship, balancing caregiving responsibilities, or reflecting on past relationships, she approaches her circumstances with honesty and resilience. She has learned from her experiences and found peace, whether partnered or not. For her, love is about the deep friendships that grow over time, the joy of shared memories, and the comfort of having a witness to her life's journey.

Embracing her Golden Years

The sixties mark a transition from decades of structure and responsibility to a season of choice, freedom, and purpose. Ms. Sixty-Something has finally retired after a long, fulfilling career, relishing the ability to work on her own terms—or not at all. Retirement brings the freedom to decide when, where, and how she wants to use her skills and experience. She can now enjoy leisurely mornings, sipping coffee and meditating before starting her day.

Retirement isn't without its adjustments. The early months were euphoric—filled with long-postponed projects, new hobbies, and the simple pleasure of unstructured time. However, after stepping away from the workforce, she feels a need to stay connected to the world of work. Choosing semi-retirement, she takes advantage of part-time opportunities to remain intellectually engaged without the pressures of a traditional 9-to-5. She finds fulfillment in sharing her knowledge while recognizing that her expertise might not always remain relevant. The flexibility of working less often and in less stressful roles is a welcome change.

> "NOW, I'M TRYING TO UNDERSTAND WHAT GOD HAS FOR ME. I'M TRYING TO CLEAR OUT PHYSICAL AND MENTAL CLUTTER, SO I'LL BE READY IF HE TELLS ME TO MOVE."

For Ms. Sixty-Something, this stage of life is about exploring, rediscovering herself, and considering how to align her time with her values and passions. It provides her time to pursue passion projects, whether mentoring, teaching, or community service. She is also choosing to embrace new ventures, like writing books, leading foundations, and exploring the world. This stage offers the best of both worlds: opportunities to stay busy and engaged without the burdens that once defined her career.

No matter where she lands in the spectrum of work and retirement, she takes pride in the journey that brought her here, grateful for the freedom to choose how she spends her days.

Getting Physical

Ms. Sixty-Something doesn't take her health for granted. Having faced major health challenges in the past, she's grateful to feel good most days. Her experiences with medical treatments have taught her the importance of advocating for herself and being proactive about her well-being.

While she acknowledges the inevitable aches and pains that come with aging—she doesn't let them stop her. She remains active and committed to a routine that works for her, whether it's walking three miles a few days a week, playing tennis, boxing, or strength training. At sixty-something, she may even choose marathon training or weightlifting because age is just a number. She knows it's not about being in perfect health but staying mobile and being consistent. She works to balance exercise with other aspects of health, like maintaining a healthy diet, even if the occasional Blue Bell ice cream calls her name.

Regular checkups and screenings are non-negotiable for Ms. Sixty-Something, as she stays vigilant with mammograms and physicals. Whether or not she's on medication, she's intentional about understanding her body and doing what's necessary to ensure she's around for her grandchildren and loved ones. Reducing stress, staying active, and caring for her mental and physical health have helped her feel better than she has in years.

> "AS YOU AGE, YOU REALIZE HOW MUCH OF A BLESSING IT IS TO HAVE GOOD HEALTH."

Though menopause and aging bring changes like weight gain and fluctuating energy levels, she embraces what sixty-something looks like today. She's committed to doing what she can to stay healthy while giving herself grace for the areas she's still working on.

Rooted in the Faith

For Ms. Sixty-Something, spirituality is a journey. She has always known God, but her understanding and relationship with Him deepened as she experienced life. She learned the true meaning of discipleship through studying the Word and discovering her spiritual gifts, which have helped her align her life with God's plans. At this stage, she can see how 'all things have worked together for her good' and finds peace and joy in trusting Him completely.

She has experienced more than one crisis of faith in her life, learning to rely on God's constancy through health challenges and career, financial, and relational struggles. Personal losses and difficult seasons have tested her, but she has been faithful. Reliance on God has fostered a profound sense of peace and joy that no circumstance can take away. She values the fellowship and accountability of being with other believers, although online worship and devotionals offer a temporary substitute when she is without a church home.

Ms. Sixty-Something starts her day with the Word, offers whispered prayers throughout and seeks God's guidance in all she does. While she desires a more intense prayer and study routine, she finds that even walking in the park with God or meditating on scripture brings her closer to Him. She strives to praise more than ask, knowing that gratitude strengthens her spirit. Her spiritual gifts motivate her to serve in ministry, and she's intentional about seeking God's direction to ensure her work is rooted in truth and not false teaching or selfish ambition.

> "GOD HAS BROUGHT ME THROUGH SO MUCH – PHYSICALLY, FINANCIALLY, AND PROFESSIONALLY. I CAN ONLY PRAISE HIM."

Ultimately, Ms. Sixty-Something seeks to live as a believer, disciple, minister, and witness to God's amazing grace while continuing to grow in her understanding of scripture and her purpose in His kingdom. She knows that He doesn't ask her to meet a standard of perfection—He simply wants her to be herself. This realization has brought freedom from anxiety and comparison, grounding her in the knowledge that she is beloved and guided by His grace. She is working to earn jewels in her crown.

Sharing Her Wisdom

For Ms. Sixty-Something, mentoring is both a calling and a natural extension of her life experiences. She views it as her role to teach, encourage, and guide younger women, whether through formal programs, spiritual ministry, or everyday interactions. She treasures the opportunity to share her wisdom, foster growth, and strengthen others' faith and confidence.

She mostly experiences mentoring opportunities that arise organically—whether someone seeks her out or God places them in her path—and she strives to approach each relationship with curiosity, humility, and a willingness to listen.

Ms. Sixty-Something's relationships with younger women often blend the personal and the practical. She mentors her daughter, advising her on child-rearing, relationships, and life's challenges. For other young women, like her goddaughter, she provides guidance on everything from managing finances and careers to navigating marriage or family dynamics. She encourages women to reflect on the bigger picture and think critically about their choices, always offering objectivity and support.

> "WHEN I WAS GROWING UP, THE OLDER WOMEN WOULD TALK IN WHISPERS OR CODE. IT'S REALLY IMPORTANT FOR OUR MENTAL AND PHYSICAL HEALTH TO SHARE OUR EXPERIENCES."

Books are another way she helps other women learn and grow. Having come from a background where books were her teachers, she shares resources like *How to Work a Room* and *How to Win Friends and Influence People*, passing on the knowledge that shaped her journey. She encourages lifelong learning and believes in equipping others with tools for growth.

Her approach to mentoring is grounded in trust, respect, and authenticity. She tries to avoid being judgmental, instead leading with curiosity and building relationships that allow women to feel safe seeking her guidance. She knows that mentoring is a two-way street—she often learns as much from those she mentors as they do from her. Whether in formal programs or informal moments, she views every interaction as an opportunity to plant seeds of wisdom and encouragement..

A Circle of Trusted Advisors

Advice and support come from a carefully curated circle of trusted individuals who have journeyed with Ms. Sixty-Something through the various seasons of her life. She relies on a mix of lifelong friends, spiritual mentors, family, and peers to provide wisdom, encouragement, and a safe space to share her heart.

Her network includes a "keeping it real" circle of friends who provide honest feedback and a listening ear. These sister-friends bring diverse perspectives, and their relationships are built on trust, longevity, and the ability to nurture each other through life's challenges. They offer her a space to be herself without judgment. Some of them came into her life during pivotal moments, like the loss of her husband, and helped her find her way back from the edge. Others are spiritual mothers—older women who have adopted her as their own and poured into her life.

> "MY CIRCLE IS VERY SMALL, AND THEY ALL BRING DIFFERENT THINGS TO THE TABLE."

She acknowledges that asking for help wasn't always easy for her. She sometimes hesitates to lean on others for fear of being a burden. She values professional counseling when needed but mainly relies on her faith, knowing that some things can only be taken to God. Because she pours into others frequently, she recognizes the importance of ensuring that she is fed emotionally and spiritually. She has no problem picking up the phone to call on her network, and she she makes time to connect with those who can pour into her.

Now, whether through peers, spiritual advisors, or lifelong friends, she is surrounded by people who encourage her, challenge her, and help her navigate life's complexities. This circle of trust ensures she has the guidance and support she needs.

Delight in Simple Things

Ms. Sixty-Something understands that happiness can be fleeting, tied to what happens, but true joy comes from the Lord. This perspective allows her to find joy in the simplest moments and blessings, big and small. She finds joy in nature—watching a rainbow, seeing a cardinal outside her window, going for a run, feeling the serenity of being near water or taking a Sunday drive. She delights in small, unexpected pleasures, like hearing her favorite song on the radio, laughing with friends, or sipping tea while listening to Roberta Flack. For Ms. Sixty-Something, these quiet, peaceful moments are reminders of God's grace and goodness.

She finds joy in her connections—seeing her husband thriving, spending quality time with friends who meet her where she is, and most of all, her children–her heart. She lights up when she sees her children thriving as adults, growing in confidence, and still sharing their lives with her. She cherishes the blessing of being a grandmother. Messages from her family in the morning, family reunions, and simply laughing and enjoying one another's company at a celebration bring her immense satisfaction. Even in the midst of loss, she holds onto memories of good times with loved ones and treasures the moments she has now.

> "I'M DELIGHTED WHEN I'M FREE TO JUST BE MYSELF, AND THE FELLOWSHIP DOESN'T HAVE TO BE ORCHESTRATED."

For Ms. Sixty-Something, happiness comes from living in the moment, staying grounded in gratitude, and finding beauty in the everyday and the extraordinary. Whether spreading cheer, holding onto fond memories, or appreciating the gift of a new day, her life is filled with joy that radiates from within.

Guidance from Older Women

The wisdom passed down to Ms. Sixty-Something from older women includes practical and spiritual insights that have shaped her life, from "***Do your life with God and let Him handle the things you can't***" to the simple reminder that "***No is a complete sentence.***" She learned to trust God, amplify others, and stop playing small, as one mentor advised her to "***see yourself the way God sees you.***" This wisdom gave her the courage to step into her purpose and use her gifts to teach, inspire, and lead.

A core principle of giving back, grounded in faith and gratitude, remains a cornerstone of her life. "***To whom much is given, much is required***," her grandmother would say, instilling a sense of responsibility to represent herself and her family with integrity. She also learned the importance of self-care, as one elder advised, "***You can't pour from an empty cup***," encouraging her to replenish herself to avoid burnout.

The call to authenticity has also been central to her journey. "***Always be your authentic self***," she was told, and to "***never let someone else tell you who you are.***" Her grandmother's wisdom echoed this, saying, "***Remember who you are and don't allow yourself to be caught up with the masses. The masses will make you forget who you are—a child of God.***" Another elder reinforced this message by advising her to "***use your voice—be seen and be brave***," encouraging her to embrace her light and not let anyone dim it.

Older women taught her the importance of advocating for herself and standing firm. "***People can't ride your back if you don't bend over***" resonated deeply, particularly in the workplace, reminding her to assert herself with confidence. Forgiveness was another profound lesson, as one mentor shared, "***Forgive yourself—you didn't know what you didn't know or what you were doing.***" This advice helped her find peace and release feelings of failure or shame, recognizing that she was doing the best she could with what she knew at the time.

These lessons reflect the powerful impact of older women's voices, reminding Ms. Sixty-Something to live authentically, nurture herself, and trust in God's plan.

Learning Forward

As Ms. Sixty-Something reflects on her journey, she is grateful for the freedom, wisdom, and joy that now define her life. Her sixties are a season of embracing purpose, shedding unnecessary burdens, and finding beauty in simplicity. She has cultivated a profound relationship with God, allowing faith to guide her and provide her peace, resilience, and clarity. She has created a life rooted in love, service, and gratitude through mentoring, serving her community, and pouring into her family.

As she navigates the road ahead, Ms. Sixty-Something understands that her best days are not behind her. She hopes to inspire others for years to come through her actions, whether by mentoring, teaching, or simply being a source of encouragement whenever possible. This is the time for embracing vulnerability and authenticity with family and friends to rekindle relationships and build deeper bonds. With the wisdom earned through decades of experience, she can confidently look to the future, knowing that she has the tools, faith, stamina, and love to continue thriving.

> *"Gray hair is a crown of glory; it is gained by living a godly life."*
> Proverbs 16:31 NLT

A Prayer for Ms. Sixty-Something

Dear God,

We thank You for the woman in her sixties who is reading this book. We thank You for her life and the fact that she is a walking testimony of your faithfulness through all the seasons of life. She has learned to wait on You and knows that it is only You that has brought her this far. We rejoice in that You have given her the grace to enjoy this season. We pray for all that You have provided and for her contentment. Let her be steadfast, immovable, always excelling in the work you have called her to knowing that her labor for you is not in vain. We ask for Your continued grace and mercy in the days, months, and years ahead. May she awaken each day seeing it as a gift and an opportunity to reflect the fruit of Your spirit - love, joy, peace, patience, kindness, goodness, faithfulness, gentleness, and self-control. We pray that others see the love of Jesus in her and ultimately want to know You too.

In the name of Your son, Jesus.

Amen

Epilogue: The Power of Woman-to-Woman Wisdom

As we reach the final pages of this book, let's reflect on the journey we have walked together—the stories of women navigating the complexities of life, growing through each decade, and embracing both the joys and challenges that shape them. Each chapter has been a testament to the power of wisdom that is passed from one woman to another.

We have seen how the guidance and instruction from the older women in our lives serve as a guiding light, offering reassurance that the road ahead, though uncertain, is never one we walk alone. Likewise, with their fresh perspectives and bold aspirations, younger women remind us that growth never stops, and neither should our willingness to evolve.

In today's world, where cultural and technological advancements are rapidly reshaping the way we connect, communicate, and find community, the need for mentorship and authentic relationships has never been greater. The rise of digital spaces has given us new opportunities to bridge generational gaps, learn from each other, and cultivate a sense of belonging, no matter where we are in life.

The simple truth is that wisdom cannot exist in isolation—it must be shared. It must be spoken, written, and, most importantly, lived out. Let us all look to apply what we learn from others and look for ways to inspire, encourage, and support those that God places in our lives. As you close this book, I invite you to take the next step. Whether that means seeking mentorship, offering guidance, or simply embracing your season with courage and faith, know that you are part of something greater.

To support this journey beyond these pages, I warmly invite you to join **The Woman-to-Woman Wisdom Circle**, our online community where women of all ages and stages come together for real, open, and vulnerable dialogue about their lived experiences. This space allows us to share our stories, uplift one another, foster mentorship, and create relationships that empower personal and professional growth.

Additionally, suppose you are ready to deepen your understanding of intergenerational mentoring and explore how to apply it in your own life. In that case, I encourage you to take advantage of the **Woman-to-Woman Study Guide: Unleashing the Power of Intergenerational Mentoring**. This guide is designed to help you reflect on your own experiences, gain insights from biblical and practical wisdom, and equip you with tools to build meaningful, cross-generational relationships.

Because, in the end, no woman should walk alone. Our stories are richer when woven together, and our lives are fuller when we lean on and learn from one another.

So, dear sister, keep building, keep growing, and keep sharing. The world needs your wisdom just as much as you need the wisdom of those who have walked before you.

Your next chapter is waiting—who will you invite to walk it with you?

A Mentoring Guide

The most notable example of a mentoring relationship in the scriptures is that of Ruth and Naomi. In the bible story, Naomi was there to guide her daughter-in-law, Ruth, as she resettled in a foreign land after losing her husband. Naomi was also a blessing to Ruth, providing support and companionship to a grieving widow and mother. It is a blessing to have someone in your life who can pour into you, and it is an awesome responsibility to take someone under your wing to pour into. The most powerful mentoring relationships are those in which we intentionally pour into each other.

In the constant evolution of what is perceived as a woman's place in society, it is essential to have women leaders, teachers, and role models to equip the generations that follow. In his second letter to Titus, Paul calls on Christian women to teach other women how to live righteously and to share practical advice for managing their households. Not only is this a task that God commands us to undertake, but He also equips us for it. Mentoring can be both formal and informal. It can involve sharing your experiences and knowledge on a variety of subjects, whether personal or professional. Most importantly, remember that as a mentor, advice is best received when it is intentional and comes from the heart.

Intentionality arises when you realize that someone else could benefit from hearing your story. If you have learned something the hard way, you can help minimize the suffering of someone else. They can learn from your experience, and you will feel good about it. Here are some things to consider before deciding to share your knowledge and experience with someone else:

- You can't teach what you don't know. Remember that it's not your responsibility to teach another adult how to do everything. However, some things you know from experience can help someone experiencing the same thing. Consider the areas in life where God has equipped you with the knowledge and know-how to share.
- Study the world of God so that you can confidently present yourself as someone who can interpret and share the truth (2 Timothy 2:15). Advice that is grounded in scripture carries a lot of weight because "the word of God is alive and active. Sharper than any double-edged sword—it judges the thoughts and attitudes of the heart" (Hebrews 4:12 NIV). If God highlights a certain topic in your life, explore it and make it a point to talk to others who have studied or experienced it.
- Consider who you are drawn to and who is drawn to you. Every woman should see herself as both older and younger. She should be able to mentor while remaining open to learning from others with more experience. Spiritual maturity and life experiences have more to do with what we have to offer and how we relate rather than chronological age. God will place people in your life who need exactly what you have to give.
- Trust is the foundation for any meaningful relationship, and it's important to remember that our reputations often precede us. Gossiping, in particular, is something to avoid. We must be

mindful of what our lifestyle and actions say about our ability to be trusted because, without the assurance of confidentiality, younger women won't be vulnerable to us.

Further, no one cares what you know if they don't know that you care. Mentoring is heart work. It requires a genuine interest in the well-being of the other person and the vulnerability to share your own personal experiences. Caring involves expressing empathy for the challenges someone else faces and acknowledging their concerns. As a mentor, you might even keep a running list of what's important to the woman you're trying to support, as well as important facts and dates.

Developing a meaningful relationship requires vulnerability and trust. Here are some questions you might ask in a conversation to demonstrate your interest in someone:

- What's the best thing about your life right now?
- What's your biggest concern right now?
- What brings you joy?
- How's your career/job going?
- How's your physical health?
- How's your spiritual life?
- How's your love life?
- How do you take care of you?

Of course, as a mentor, you must be prepared to share your own answers and be open to learning as well. Remember, the relationship should be mutually beneficial and enjoyable.

It is important to note that not everyone is comfortable asking for a mentor. So first, take a few minutes to look back on a relationship that you had with an older woman who helped teach you about any particular aspect of your life. Consider how the relationship began, what you received from her, and what she got out of the relationship. Then, allow the Holy Spirit to guide you as you open your heart and set your intentions on becoming a woman who supports another woman on her journey through the various stages of life.

FINDING A MENTOR

Suppose you are seeking a mentoring relationship with an older woman. In that case, you should keep in mind that she will be more receptive if she gets a sense that she is making a positive difference and receives the occasional expression of appreciation. To pique her interest in a relationship with you, first:

- Consider what you need or want from the relationship.
- Consider who in your social or professional network has experience in your areas of interest or is doing something you want to do.
- Build rapport based on shared interests and values to develop comfort and trust.
- Have the courage to ask for help, but don't ask for or expect special favors
- Be purposeful and pleasant, and have interesting or challenging topics to discuss.
- Be respectful of her time

Overcoming Potential Challenges in Mentoring

Bridging Generational Gaps: Different communication styles and expectations can be challenging.

> Tip: Be curious and adaptable. Use shared goals to bridge the gap and actively learn from each other's perspectives.

Navigating Miscommunication: Misunderstandings can strain the relationship.

Tip: Practice active listening and clarify intentions. Regularly check in to ensure alignment.

Maintaining Engagement: Life changes or scheduling conflicts can impact consistency in connecting.

Tip: Be flexible with meetings and use tools like video calls, emails, or messaging to stay connected.

Setting Boundaries: Be wary of overstepping or unclear boundaries.

Tip: Discuss and agree on boundaries early. Revisit them if needed to maintain mutual respect.

Dealing with Disappointments: Unrealized expectations or mismatched goals can fracture a relationship.

Solution: Address concerns honestly and respectfully. Decide if adjustments or a natural conclusion to the relationship is best.

Conclusion

By fostering meaningful intergenerational mentoring relationships, we can uplift one another as women and build a legacy of shared wisdom and growth. Let this guide inspire you to embark on or deepen your mentoring journey. Remember, a mutually beneficial relationship is the goal; therefore, both parties should practice trust-building interpersonal skills. Whether the relationship lasts for a season or a lifetime, the rewards are well worth the time and effort.

Acknowledgments

We extend our deepest gratitude to the incredible women who generously shared their stories, experiences, and wisdom as part of this project. Your candid reflections on the joys, challenges, and lessons from life have provided invaluable insights into the evolving journey of womanhood. Through your vulnerability, you have enriched this book and offered a powerful testament to resilience, growth, and the beauty of embracing each stage of life. Thank you for allowing us to learn from your journeys and inspiring future generations of women to navigate their paths with courage, faith, and grace.

We want to acknowledge contributions from each of the following women who we spoke with over the past year:

Valerie Adair	Sylvia Chester
Kayla Baker	Jennifer Chester
Robyn Brandon	Cassandra Christian
Janice Character	Samantha Conyers

Lisa Critchlow
Taryn Cumbo
Lindsay Davis
Denise Day
Chanel Derricott
Valeria Edmonds
Rachael Edmonds
Kia Farlough
Simone Fennell
Cheryl Fleming
Gayle Giles
Kim Goodall
Germaine Grinkley
Karen Hayes
Denise Hill
Andora Hinton
Laura Knights
Jillian Lopez
Andonnia Maiben
Robyn McCoy
Sybil Miller
Tiffany Million
Philecia Moore

Micah Moore
Reyna Northcutt
Shari Pace
Keiwana Perryman
Michaela R
Gail Boyd Rogers
Bonitta Saulsberry
Alicia Saulsberry
Daija Saulsberry
Jymae Saulsberry
Jarietta Saulsberry
Taylor Shaw
Shavonne Spencer
Felicia Strickland
Jane Talford
Rosalyn Taylor
Nickeisha Thomas
Tamika Tyson
Amy Walker
Lateesha Watkins
Tiffany Wiggins
Kisheena Williams
Sharmon Williams

About the Authors

Valeria and Rachael Edmonds are a purpose-driven mother and daughter duo who undertook this writing project to scale the positive intergenerational mentorship experience they have shared as adult women.

Dr. Valeria Edmonds is a retired global HR leader whose calling is ministering to other women by sharing her life lessons through mentoring, coaching, teaching, writing, and speaking. She is passionate about helping younger women thrive personally and professionally as they seek to be their best selves. As a Christian, she brings a practical and relevant perspective to how we can walk a godly life by faith, as instructed in Titus 2:3-5.

Rachael Edmonds, M.Ed., has professional experience in higher education, supporting students with their college journeys. Her passion is helping others to learn and grow. She has enjoyed learning from the older women in her life and wants the richness of that experience to be available to others. Rachael's spiritual gift of discernment helps her to empathize with those she mentors. She enjoys bringing people together to share experiences that inspire and refresh the soul.

www.ingramcontent.com/pod-product-compliance
Lightning Source LLC
LaVergne TN
LVHW061048070526
838201LV00074B/5215